Sports Illustrated
FOOTBALL:
DEFENSE

THE SPORTS ILLUSTRATED LIBRARY

BOOKS ON TEAM SPORTS

Baseball
Basketball
Football: Defense
Football: Offense
Pitching
Soccer

BOOKS ON INDIVIDUAL SPORTS

Bowling
Cross-Country Skiing
Golf
Racquetball
Skiing
Tennis
Track: The Running Events

Tumbling
Women's Gymnastics I:
    The Floor Exercise Event
Women's Gymnastics II:
    The Vaulting, Balance Beam
    and Uneven Parallel Bars Events

BOOKS ON WATER SPORTS

Boardsailing
Canoeing
Scuba Diving

SPECIAL BOOKS

Backpacking
Strength Training

Sports Illustrated
FOOTBALL:
DEFENSE

by BUD WILKINSON

Illustrations by Robert Handville

REVISED EDITION

PERENNIAL LIBRARY

HARPER & ROW, PUBLISHERS, New York
Cambridge, Philadelphia, San Francisco, London
Mexico City, São Paulo, Singapore, Sydney

SPORTS ILLUSTRATED FOOTBALL: DEFENSE *(Revised Edition)*. Copyright © 1986 by Time Inc. All rights reserved. Printed in the United States of America. No part of this book may be used or reproduced in any manner whatsoever without written permission except in the case of brief quotations embodied in critical articles and reviews. For information address Harper & Row, Publishers, Inc., 10 East 53rd Street, New York, N.Y. 10022. Published simultaneously in Canada by Fitzhenry & Whiteside Limited, Toronto.

Library of Congress Cataloging in Publication Data

Wilkinson, Bud, 1916–
    Sports illustrated football, defense.

    (The Sports illustrated library)
    1. Football—Defense. 2. Football—Coaching.
I. Sports illustrated (Time, inc.) II. Title.
III. Series.
GV951.18.W55   1986   796.332'2   84–48203
ISBN 0–06–055007–4   86 87 88 89 90 MVP 10 9 8 7 6 5 4 3 2 1
ISBN 0–06–091266–9 (pbk.)   86 87 88 89 90 MVP 10 9 8 7 6 5 4 3 2 1

Sports Illustrated
FOOTBALL:
DEFENSE

by BUD WILKINSON

Illustrations by Robert Handville

REVISED EDITION

PERENNIAL LIBRARY

HARPER & ROW, PUBLISHERS, New York
Cambridge, Philadelphia, San Francisco, London
Mexico City, São Paulo, Singapore, Sydney

Photo credits:

For *Sports Illustrated*—Manny Millan: pp. 3, 40, 132; Heinz Kluetmeier: pp. 8, 21 (right), 24, 56, 146, 152, 164,172; Walter Iooss, Jr.: p. 12; Peter Read Miller; p. 21 (left); Roy Hobson: p. 64; Andy Hayt: pp. 66, 122, 126 (top), 162, 174; Jerry Wachter: p. 86; Phil Huber: p. 104; Manny Rubio: p. 110; Tony Triolo: p. 126 (bottom); Tony Tomsic: p. 154.
Wide World Photos © by Associated Press: p. 14.

All illustrations by Robert Handville.

All diagrams by Frank Ronan.

Library of Congress Cataloging in Publication Data

Wilkinson, Bud, 1916–
    Sports illustrated football, defense.

    (The Sports illustrated library)
    1. Football—Defense. 2. Football—Coaching.
I. Sports illustrated (Time, inc.) II. Title.
III. Series.
GV951.18.W55   1986   796.332'2   84–48203
ISBN 0–06–055007–4   86 87 88 89 90 MVP 10 9 8 7 6 5 4 3 2 1
ISBN 0–06–091266–9 (pbk.) 86 87 88 89 90 MVP 10 9 8 7 6 5 4 3 2 1

Contents

Keys to Diagrams

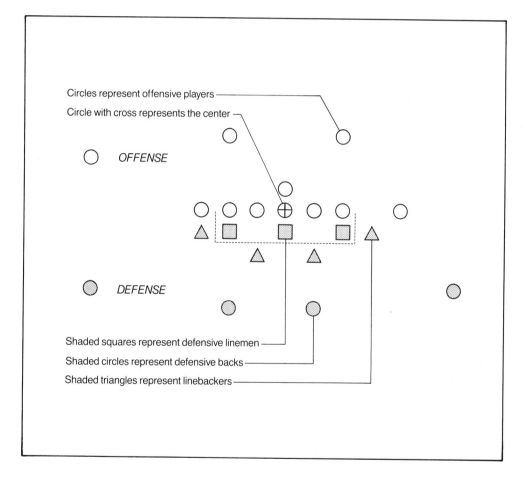

Circles represent offensive players

Circle with cross represents the center

OFFENSE

DEFENSE

Shaded squares represent defensive linemen

Shaded circles represent defensive backs

Shaded triangles represent linebackers

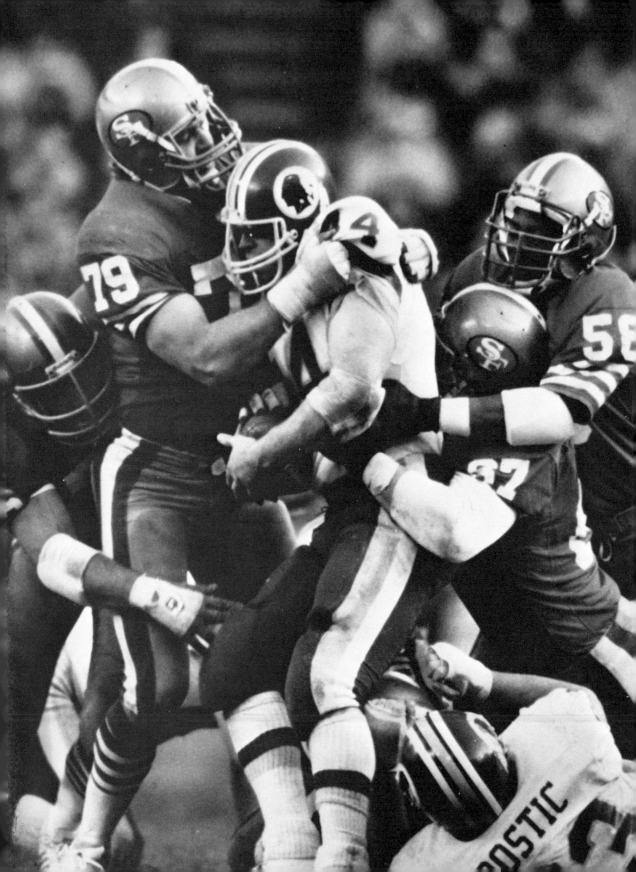

Introduction

When I played football for the National Champion Golden Gophers of the University of Minnesota in the mid-1930s, and for most of the years I coached at the University of Oklahoma, football was a one-platoon game. The same players were required to play both offense and defense.

In recent years, through rule changes, football has become a two-platoon game and, in reality, a football team today is two separate teams: One team plays only offense, the other plays only defense. (Either offensive or defensive players may make up the personnel for the special teams, those units, offensive and defensive, used on kickoffs, punts, extra points and field goals.)

This clear division of a squad into two separate teams has given fans and spectators a greater appreciation of the value and importance of defense. An offensive team may be good and score scads of points, but if the opponents score more points, the inadequate defensive team has been responsible for a loss.

Though the media and fans are beginning to recognize great defensive players—men like Ronnie Lott, strong safety of the San Francisco 49ers, and Lawrence Taylor, linebacker of the New York Giants—the fact remains that offensive players

9

"If your opponent does not score, you cannot lose."

are still considered the "stars" in both college and professional football. Indeed, one only has to look at the salaries paid to pro quarterbacks compared with those paid defensive players to see that the glamour of the game remains with the offensive players.

In spite of this disparity, it is also a fact that the defense wins or loses football games. Proof? Look at the San Francisco 49ers.

During the first three years Bill Walsh coached the 49ers, the team averaged almost the same number of points on offense: In 1979, 19.3 per game; in 1980, 20 per game; and in 1981, 23.2 per game. In his first year as coach, 1979, the defense gave up an average of 26 points per game, and in 1980 they surrendered 25.9 points per game. In 1981, the season in which the 49ers won the Super Bowl, they surrendered only 15.6 points per game. It doesn't take a computer to understand the significance of those statistics.

From a tactical and strategic standpoint, football is divided into three phases: the offense; the defense; and the kicking game. Execution in all three of these phases must usually be good for the team to win. Without question, however, defense is the most important phase of the game. Why? Consider:

1. If your opponent does not score, you cannot lose. The worst you can do is tie.

2. There are two ways in which an offensive team can get the ball: when their defensive teammates stop the opponent's offense or force a punt or a turnover, and when their defensive teammates allow the opponent to score. Needless to say, any team that leads the league in the number of kickoffs it receives will not have a winning record. To win, a team must get possession of the ball by stopping its opponent and forcing a punt.

Each of the three phases of football requires athletic ability, but most coaches agree that playing effective defense takes far more physical and mental ability than the other two phases. Primarily, this is because playing defense calls for immediate response to an unknown situation. Offense is, by contrast, a relatively static situation in which players execute precisely defined assignments.

On defense, all players are confronted with the following problems on every play:

1. *Where to line up.* Since different offensive formations have different areas of strength, defensive men are never sure of the position they must take until the offensive team has taken its alignment. This requires the defense to adjust to meet the strength of the offensive formation being used.

2. *The defense is handicapped at the start of each play.* The offensive team knows when the ball will be snapped, and by proper execution of the starting count it can beat the defensive team to the punch. Thus, when the play begins, the defensive team is momentarily behind.

3. *Offensive plays are designed to mislead the defense.* All of the maneuvers and fakes of the offensive team are executed to fool the defense regarding the real point of attack. If a defensive player is drawn out of position, even for a split second, the offense has gained another great advantage.

To summarize: The defensive player does not know *where* he will line up. He will be slightly *behind* at the start of every play. And after surrendering these two advantages, he must *ignore the fakes of the offense,* move to the ball, and stop the play. All this requires tremendous athletic ability.

By way of contrast, the offensive player knows before the play begins:

1. Exactly where he will line up
2. Exactly when the ball will be snapped
3. Precisely what his assignment will be

Thus, the offensive situation requires little in the way of reaction. Given average ability, a boy can be taught, through proper practice and repetitive drills, to be an effective offensive player. Because of the difficult physical and mental reactions that are necessary to play defense, however, it is very difficult for a boy who does not possess outstanding athletic ability to become an effective defensive player.

That raises interesting coaching problems. How do you place your players in position? Who will be your offensive linemen, defensive linemen, linebackers, offensive backs, wide receivers . . . ? The judgment involved in these decisions is most difficult for the coach.

Because of the glamour of offense, the natural coaching reaction is to place the best athletes on the offensive unit and then piece together the defensive unit from the talent that remains. If defense *is* the most important phase of the game, though, and if it *does* require superior athletic ability, the best athletes should be assigned to the defensive unit. The offensive team would consequently be manned by the most effective athletes remaining after the defensive team has been set—with the exception of one position on offense, quarterback, which should be filled at the start.

Physical factors are vital in the assignment of squad members to various positions. The question arises as to whether or not speed and quickness are more important than height and weight. Generally, it is more important on

On defense, the guiding rule is: hit or be hit.

defense to have speed and quickness than height and weight, although any coach would love to have a squad full of large, fast, *and* agile players. Defensive players must hit, react, and then use their speed to move to the ball. Football, in its purest sense, is a game of reaction and speed of foot, and defensive players who lack quickness and speed surrender the basic ingredients of successful defensive play.

The mental attitude of defensive players is also very important. They must be highly aggressive—physical fighters. One of the axioms of football is that on each play "you either hit or get hit." The players who "get hit" the most are the ones who lose. Since the defensive team is behind at the start of the play because of the offense's knowledge of the starting count, it must be aggressive enough to hit, fight, and overcome that disadvantage with its willpower, determination, and physical skills. The defense must be prepared to "out-hit" its opponents if it expects to stop them.

This book explains the fundamentals and theory of defensive football for young players, coaches at the cub football or junior high level, and those fans who desire a more complete understanding of the game.

1

Components of the Defensive Team

When football was a one-platoon game, every man was required to play both offense and defense. Half of practice time was devoted to offense, half to defense. This limited practice time forced teams to use much simpler patterns of defense than are used today.

When I played for the University of Minnesota in the one-platoon era, almost every team used the same defense. The offensive ends played defensive end. The offensive tackles played defensive tackle. The offensive guards played defensive guard. The center and the fullback played as defensive linebackers. The halfbacks played defensive halfback. And the quarterback played defensive safety.

In those days, almost every offensive team used the single-wing formation. The basic play from the single-wing was the off-tackle play in which the end and wingback double-teamed the defensive tackle, the guard and quarterback (blocking back) double-teamed the end out, and the fullback and the remaining guard led the ball-carrier through the hole.

From that basic play, offensive teams also used reverses to the wingback and trap plays and wedge plays against the interior defensive linemen

15

Old-time one-platoon football was characterized by simple offensive running plays and simpler defensive patterns.

One-Platoon Football

Blocking back
Quarterback

Halfback

Halfback

DEFENSE

Center

Fullback

End

Tackle

Guard

Guard

Tackle

End

End   Tackle   Guard   Center   Guard   Tackle   End

OFFENSE

Quarterback
Blocking back

Wingback

Halfback   Fullback
Tailback

One-platoon football's basic offensive and defensive formations virtually mirrored each other.

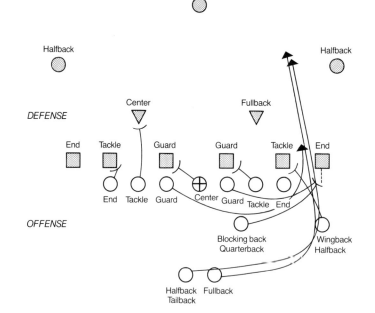

Blocking back
Quarterback

Halfback

Halfback

DEFENSE

Center

Fullback

End   Tackle   Guard   Guard   Tackle   End

End   Tackle   Guard   Center   Guard   Tackle   End

OFFENSE

Blocking back
Quarterback

Wingback
Halfback

Halfback   Fullback
Tailback

The off-tackle play from the single wing
In the days of one-platoon football, this was the most common play run from the single wing.

and linebackers. Sure, teams did throw the football, but almost always it was designed to "loosen" the defensive linebackers and secondary so they could not come up as quickly against the basic running attack. Essentially, offensive teams expected to win by running the ball, and they used pass plays only as a surprise.

The running attack was considered the brave, manly way of making yardage. Jock Sutherland, the great coach of University of Pittsburgh teams in the 1930s, stressed the point by stating that in his opinion "a forward pass play is not only cowardly—it is immoral."

In those days, the defensive teams played exactly the same defense on every play. The game was rugged and hard-hitting. It was not sophisticated, offensively or defensively.

The "T" formation came into being through Clark Shaughnessy when he coached Stanford University just before World War II. The formation was first used effectively in the NFL by the Chicago Bears under Coach George Halas and their great quarterback, Sid Luckman. When the war ended, a rapid transformation took place. Almost all teams changed from the basic single-wing formation to the new "T." This offensive pattern provided far greater deception for the offense and running plays developed much more quickly. Also, the quarterback ceased being a blocker. Instead, he became strictly a ball-handler and passer.

The single-wing had been a compact formation. The defense needed to defend a lateral front of only about 14 yards. Pass receivers were part of the compact formation, and it took them considerable time to get downfield and to the outside while running their pass patterns.

As the passing game developed and became as important as the running attack in moving the ball, coaches recognized the value of detaching receivers from the compact formation and using them as wide receivers. Also, the offensive linemen in the "split-T" formation took "large spaces" between each other —that is, they did not line up close together.

Those two developments required the defensive team to defend the field from sideline to sideline, instead of across a narrow front. Since the same men were still playing both offense and defense, their defensive skills were limited by both practice time and by the physical requirements they needed to play on offense.

With the advent of two-platoon football, the game became much more sophisticated. Today, players are able to spend all their practice time learning and honing their skills as either offensive or defensive men. In effect, this doubles their practice time and enables coaches to use much more complicated defenses.

The Evolution of the Passing Game

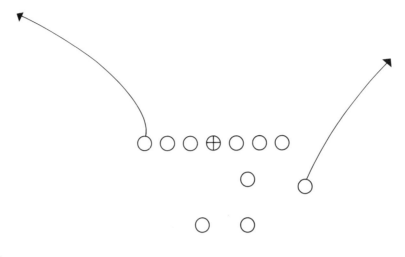

A

In the single wing (shown here) and the earliest "T" formation, receivers needed a great deal of time to run wide pass patterns (A). However, as the T formation evolved, one end and one back were moved to the outside as "wide receivers." The passing game was changed forever (B).

B

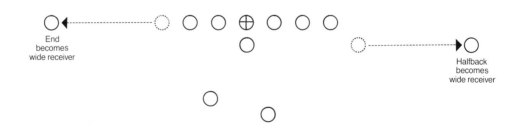

The T-Formation

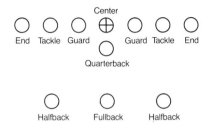

Note the spacing between players—wider than that for the single wing.

The Split-T Formation

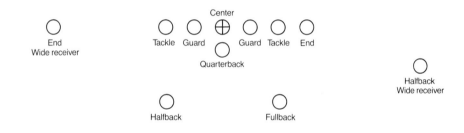

The "split-T" with detached wide receivers. In this formation, the defense was forced to defend the field both from sideline to sideline and deep down field.

A dramatic example of the change which the two-platoon system has brought to football is a wide receiver like Cliff Branch of the Los Angeles Raiders. Cliff runs the 100-yard dash in 9.4 seconds. He is 5′10″ and weighs about 170 pounds. For years in the NFL, he has been a dominant receiver. Were football a one-platoon game, however, it is doubtful that he could have become a football player: He would have remained a track man since he lacked the physical make-up to be an effective defensive player.

There are a wide variety of defensive alignments used in modern football. Within those defensive patterns, however, the components are always the same:

1. Down (or interior) linemen
2. Linebackers
3. Secondary men

A few years ago, there was a fourth defensive position—defensive end. Men who played defensive end rushed the passer and defended against running plays. As the offensive passing game became more sophisticated, men who played defensive end were forced to *cover* pass receivers in addition to rushing the passer and stopping runs. Men who lacked the speed to cover receivers could no longer be effective defenders.

In today's game, men who formerly played end on a five-, six-, or seven-man defensive line have become linebackers. Defensive ends are down linemen who play on the end of a three- or four-man defensive line.

DEFENSIVE POSITIONS

Down Linemen

They must be big, and they must have great arm and leg strength. Their primary defensive responsibilities are to control the offensive men in their area, to resist the offensive blockers at the line of scrimmage, and then to move to the ball.

The down linemen normally include two tackles and two guards, or two tackles and a nose guard. They take their position within a yard of the line of scrimmage from offensive tackle to offensive tackle.

Position of the down linemen
Defensive down linemen take their positions within the area outlined.

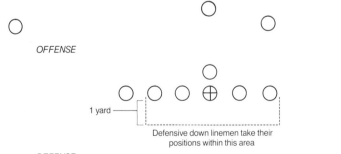

Stance of the down linemen
Most down linemen take their stance with one or both hands on the ground (A).

A few coaches, however, feel that the semi-erect stance (B) gives the defensive lineman a better view of the action as it develops.

The term "down" derives from the fact that they have one or both hands on the ground as they take their stance. A recent development in defensive play used by teams has the "down" linemen who play over the offensive tackles assuming a semi-erect stance rather than a stance with one or both hands on the ground. Coaches using this technique believe it allows their interior linemen to get a better view of the action in the offensive backfield and to move more quickly and precisely as they play the opponents immediately in front of them.

Linebackers

Linebacker is the most difficult position on the defensive team. Linebackers must be strong enough to neutralize any offensive player trying to block them, but they also must be fast enough to cover a tight end or running back who is a potential receiver on a pass play. The position requires both strength and speed, a rare combination.

Linebackers usually take their position 2 to 5 yards behind the line of scrimmage, opposite the offensive ends or at some position to the inside of them.

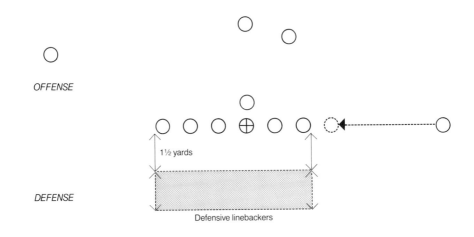

OFFENSE

DEFENSE

1½ yards

Defensive linebackers

Position of the linebackers
Defensive linebackers take their positions in the shaded area shown here.

The rules prohibit interior offensive linemen from moving farther than one yard downfield on pass plays. By lining up at least 1½ yards behind the line of scrimmage and watching (or "keying" on) the offensive linemen, the backers get a quick indication of whether the play is a run or a pass since the offensive linemen cannot move in to block them on pass plays.

Secondary

Secondary men are divided into two groups—the cornerbacks and the safeties. The cornerbacks are the outside defenders in the secondary. While they must be able to "support" against running plays, their primary requirement is the speed and ability to cover pass receivers all over the field.

The safeties play as the *strong safety,* to the side of the offensive tight end, and the *free safety,* to the side of the split-end wide receiver. These men must possess great speed to cover pass receivers deep downfield, but they must also be able to support quickly and effectively against running plays.

Some teams use a free safety and a "monster" back. The monster man is in reality a strong safety moved forward to a spot about 4 yards from the line of scrimmage. From this position he can support more quickly against running plays.

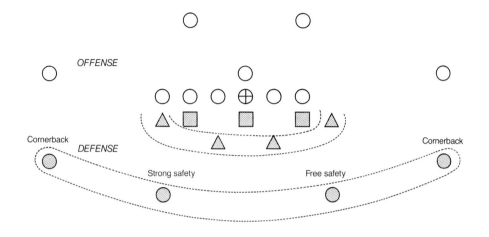

The position of the free safety as "monster man"

Note that the "monster defense," which takes its name from the position of the free safety, is in reality an overshift to the wide side of the field.

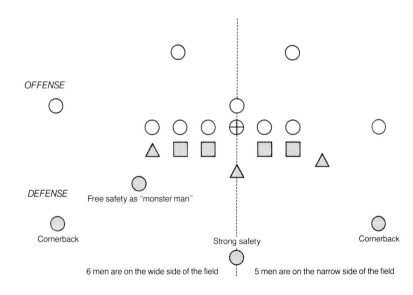

The Fundamentals

Defensive men in proximity to offensive players—interior linemen or linebackers playing on the line of scrimmage—hit their opponents with enough force to neutralize their charge, control the opponents to avoid being blocked, locate the ball, and then move to it. To do all these things in a few seconds takes great athletic ability, and to do them consistently throughout a game takes the skills of a Leroy Selmon of the Tampa Bay Buccaneers, a Randy White of the Dallas Cowboys, or a Doug English of the Detroit Lions.

DEFENSIVE KEYS

Men who take their position farther than 1½ yards from any offensive player—linebackers and secondary men—must "read" or "key" as the ball is snapped. These terms mean watching one or two offensive players whose movement at the start of the play usually indicates the type of play to be run.

Since football rules prevent the offensive tackles, guards, or center from being more than a yard across the line of scrimmage on forward pass plays, the moment an ineligible receiver moves

25

Randy White's ability to fight off attackers and move to the ball makes him one of the best defensive players in the NFL.

Incorrect and Correct Stepping Technique
When Keying on an Offensive Lineman

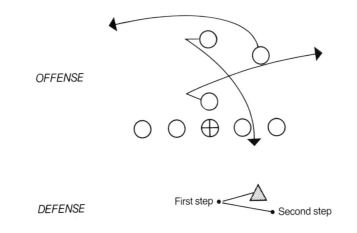

OFFENSE

DEFENSE

First step ●◀── △

● Second step

A

(A) The linebacker, fooled by the quarterback and running backs, steps in the wrong direction. His second step puts him back where he started. He has wasted two steps.

B

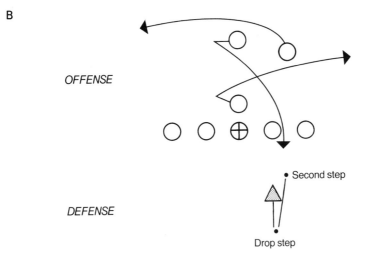

OFFENSE

DEFENSE

● Second step

●
Drop step

(B) The smart linebacker takes a short drop step, quickly reads the movement of the lineman, then moves efficiently to stop the play.

farther than a yard downfield, the defense can safely assume that the play is a run and close in to stop the ballcarrier.

By watching the offensive linemen and reading the following keys, linebackers and secondary men can learn the type of play and its direction:

1. Offensive linemen downfield means the play is a run.

2. Offensive linemen pulling out either to the left or right indicates that the play is going in that direction. (Occasionally, however, the linemen may pull in the wrong direction to mislead the defense.)

3. Offensive linemen drop-stepping back to execute a pass-protection block indicates that the play will be a pass. (On occasion, though, they will move in that way when the play is a draw play or a screen pass.)

It is important that men who are keying do not become overanxious and move too quickly in the wrong direction. A step in the wrong direction requires another step to put the player back in his original position. Thus, two steps have been wasted, delaying the defensive player's ability to get to the ball. And since football is a game of inches and split seconds, that can sometimes mean the difference between victory and defeat.

To avoid moving in the wrong direction, linebackers and secondary men should take a short drop step with either foot while they read the movement of the offensive linemen. By doing that, they can hold their position until they are sure of the type of play being run, instead of advancing the wrong way.

Keying on an Offensive Lineman

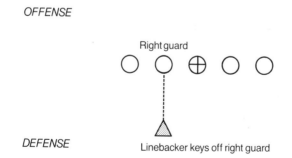

OFFENSE

Right guard

DEFENSE   Linebacker keys off right guard

The ready position: In this situation, the linebacker keys on the offensive right guard.

Keying on an Offensive Lineman (cont.)

In these situations, the linebacker (#43, dark jersey) keys on #75, an offensive lineman.

Situation #1: The offensive lineman charges across the line of scrimmage. The play is a run. The linebacker penetrates.

Situation #2: The lineman pulls to the left. The linebacker moves with the play to the left.

Situation #3: The lineman pulls to the right. The linebacker moves to the right.

Situation #4: The lineman drops back to make a pass-protection block. The linebacker drops back in preparation for the possible pass in his zone.

BLOCK PROTECTION

The most important fundamental for all defensive players is "block protection." To move to the ball, defensive players must keep their legs free. If an offensive man is successful in getting to the defender's legs or body, he can effectively prevent the defender from making further movement in the direction of the ball.

Proper block protection requires that, immediately before contact with an offensive blocker, the defensive player have his feet spread about the width of his shoulders, his knees bent and his hands and arms dangling down to protect his knees, thighs, and waist. From that position, the defender can deliver a blow with his hands, arms, and shoulders to knock the offensive player away from his legs and body and thereby maintain freedom of movement.

The defensive player cannot protect properly if he does not bend his knees enough to lower his center of gravity and enable him to deliver an up-and-out blow. His hands and arms are now so high that the blocker can get under the block protection to the defender's legs and body to make an effective block.

Another block-protection error is to have the feet too close together. That eliminates the balance and body control needed to fight the opponent, and it, too, raises the defender's center of gravity.

Protecting Against the Block:
Correct and Incorrect Positions

In the correct block-protection hitting position (A), the defensive player is ready for any move an offensive blocker makes on him.

A

(B) shows what happens when a defensive man stands too upright. The blocker has gotten to his body and has stopped him.

In (C), the defender's stance is too narrow. He's lost all leverage for fighting off the blocker.

C

PROPER ANGLE OF PURSUIT

After diagnosing the play and locating the ball, all defensive players must move to the ball on the proper "angle of pursuit." The correct angle is the course the defender must take to meet the ballcarrier at the earliest possible moment.

The relative speed of the two men is the controlling factor. The faster the ballcarrier, the further downfield the defensive lineman or linebacker must move to tackle him. The slower the ballcarrier and the faster the pursuer, the more the defender can move directly at the carrier.

It is of paramount importance that no defenders get behind the ballcarrier by penetrating and end up having to chase the play.

Instead, the defenders must move on the proper angle of pursuit to get in front of the ballcarrier at the earliest possible moment.

Proper angle of pursuit
The defender (light jersey) stays in front of the ballcarrier and stops him at the line of scrimmage.

Improper angle of pursuit
By penetrating too soon, the defender (white jersey) has gotten behind the ballcarrier, who easily eludes him.

Having closed on the ballcarrier, the defensive player is now ready to make the tackle. As he approaches the area of contact, the defender should bend his knees to assume a balanced base—the hitting position. His feet should be spread approximately as wide as his shoulders. His eyes must focus on the target, which should be the belt buckle of the ballcarrier.

Many running backs have excellent balance and an uncanny ability to fake with their head, eyes, shoulders, arms, and even legs. But it is difficult to fake with the belt buckle. Even the elusive Tony Dorsett will be where his belt buckle is. And by concentrating only on the belt buckle, the tackler will avoid being faked.

Having assumed the hitting position and keeping his spine straight, his head up and his eyes fixed firmly on the belt buckle, the tackler closes on the ballcarrier. At the moment of contact, he drives his helmet through the ball as his hands and arms encircle the hips of the ballcarrier. By driving the helmet

The Tackler's Target

A tackler's target is the ballcarrier's belt buckle.

The tackler should not look at the entire ballcarrier.

Making the Tackle

The tackle begins with the tackler zeroing in on the ballcarrier's belt buckle (A).

A

At the moment of contact, the tackler's helmet butts the ball, and his hands and arms encircle the ballcarrier's hips (B).

B

The tackler lifts the ballcarrier off the ground (C) . . . and drives him back (D).

C

D

A well-aimed punch at the ball is
another legal method for causing
a fumble.

through the ball (when it is held at the runner's side), the tackler may knock the ball loose and cause a fumble. The muscles of the tackler's legs, back, and arms lift the ballcarrier off the ground and drive him back so that he cannot fall forward for extra yardage.

The tackler must *never* close his eyes when about to make contact. In the vicinity of the tackler, the ballcarrier will be using his most violent evasive moves. If the tackler closes his eyes, he is "blind" and hands his adversary a monumental advantage.

If he cannot see the ballcarrier, the defender has no chance of making a clean tackle.

The Side-Body Tackle

When the ballcarrier is moving at an angle to the outside and it is impossible for the tackler to meet him head on, the defensive player should use the side-body tackle. Again, the target is the belt buckle. At the moment of contact, the tackler assumes the hitting position. He drives his head and shoulders in front of the ballcarrier, grasps the man with both arms, and then rolls with the ballcarrier as they fall forward. If the tackler's head is not driven across in front of the ballcarrier, the carrier's legs, almost certainly stronger than the defender's arms, will enable the carrier to break the tackle and continue downfield. Arm tackling is risky business at best; against the likes of a John Riggins or an Eric Dickerson it is futile.

The Side-Body Tackle

A

(A) shows the point of contact for the side-body tackle. Once contact has been made, the tackler encircles the ballcarrier's hips as in a normal tackle (B), but then rolls with the carrier to complete the tackle (C).

B

C

Arm Tackling

In (A), the tackler commits the un-pardonable error of using only his arms to try to tackle the ballcarrier. Result: The ballcarrier breaks free (B).

A

B

HOW TO RECOVER A FUMBLE

In high school and college football, a fumble or loose ball cannot be advanced. The player can simply recover possession of the ball for his team. In professional football, the rules differ and a fumble or loose ball can be picked up and advanced by the man making the recovery. If the fumbled ball is in the open and the man making the recovery is positive he has time to pick up the ball and advance it, he should pick it up and run with it, trying even for a touchdown.

But the man making the recovery must be positive he can pick up the ball cleanly without bobbling it and risking another fumble.

When a fumble occurs in high school or college games (or in a professional game where the player is not positive he can pick up the ball and run with it), the nearby player should fall on the ball, encircling it with his body and arms. The player making the recovery should expect that his opponents will try to take the ball away from him—in fact, there is usually a pile-up of offensive and defensive players when a fumble occurs. The referee does not rule who actually has the ball until all the players are untangled and he can clearly see which man is in possession. By properly covering the ball and holding it tight until the referee rules on possession, the player making the recovery can maintain possession of the ball for his team.

How not to recover a fumble
By scooping at the ball, the player risks bobbling it further.

Proper Technique for Recovering a Fumble

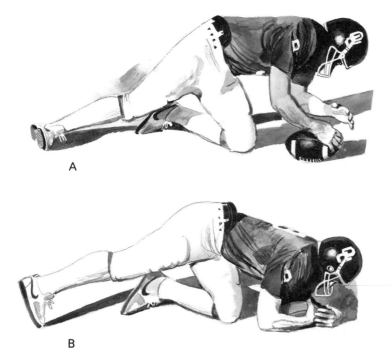

A

B

The player literally falls on the ball and draws it close to his body.

So much for defensive fundamentals. If a young player is ever going to shine playing defense, he should practice these fundamentals until they become second nature to him. But practice alone is not enough. The gifted defensive player is the one who concentrates on every play, as if every movement, every hit, every tackle he makes is *the* movement, *the* hit, *the* tackle that saves the game. And in a way he's right, because the moment he lets his concentration flag, the moment he naps on the job—that's when the opposition can score.

The best defensive players are preternaturally alert.

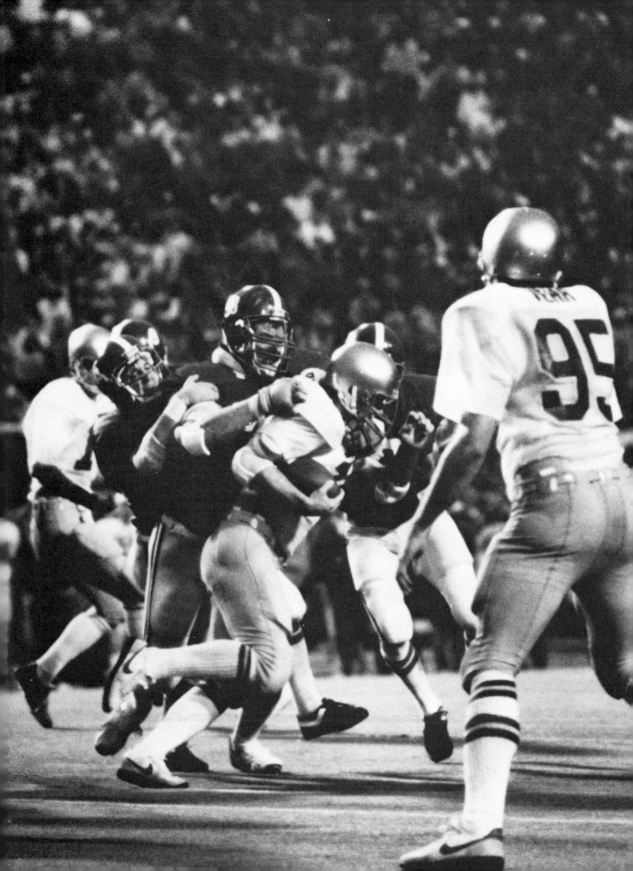

Play of the Down Linemen

Interior linemen must have quickness, strength, and size. After all, it is their mission to control the line of scrimmage. They must have sufficient size and strength to be able to defend themselves from the charge of their offensive opponents and not be driven back. They must also have sufficient quickness to move to the ball after they have avoided their opponents' initial blocks.

It is one of football's truisms that the team that controls the line of scrimmage wins the game. Defensive linemen are responsible for controlling the line of scrimmage for their team.

STANCE

There are two standard stances for interior linemen, the three-point stance, with one hand on the ground, and the four-point stance, with both hands on the ground. Other than the position of the hands, the stances are identical. To assume either stance, the lineman should spread his feet to about the width of the shoulders, bend his knees, and coil his legs. The hips should be slightly lower than the shoulders, and the torso should be stretched forward with a reasonable amount of

41

The principal job of the defensive line is to control the line of scrimmage.

Defensive Stances

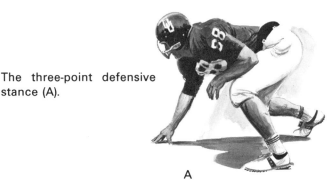

The three-point defensive stance (A).

The four-point defensive stance (B).

weight resting on the hand or hands on the ground. The ground hand (or hands) should be open, with the weight spread evenly on the fingertips.

As previously noted, some coaches occasionally have their interior linemen play in a semi-erect stance. This position should be taken with the feet spread about the width of the shoulders. One foot is dropped back slightly to give the defensive player an opportunity to step and strike a sharp blow against the opponent who charges him.

Usually the down lineman will crowd the line of scrimmage to get as close to the opponent as the rules allow. On occasion, however, if the defensive man has somewhat slow reflexes or if he has an assignment to "read" the defense as he charges, he may play back off the line of scrimmage. This gives him a moment to read his key properly before the offensive player can make contact.

In most defensive alignments, the interior linemen are given the responsibility of defeating one opponent and making sure that the opponent does not block them to a particular side. While being ready to defeat the primary opponent, however, the defender should watch the other two offensive linemen in his immediate area, since any one of the three may attack him. By watching the three men in his area, the lineman gets a fast key to the play being run and is ready to fight the block of the man who is attacking him.

Defensive Preparation for Attack

The defensive lineman (dark jersey) sees all three men and is prepared for attack by any of them.

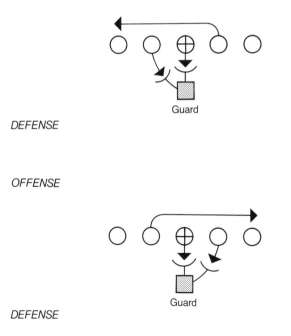

OFFENSE

Guard

DEFENSE

OFFENSE

Guard

DEFENSE

Here the defender uses his right forearm to protect his left side.

DEFENDER PROTECTS ONE SIDE

To defeat his opponent and protect his left side, the down lineman charges the opponent at the snap of the ball. He steps with his right foot and drives his right forearm under the chest of the offensive blocker, keeping the blocker's head to the inside of his right upper arm. He then raises the offensive blocker with his shoulder and forearm, forces the man back, frees himself, and moves to the ball.

To protect his right, the defender steps with his left foot and hits with his left arm and shoulder.

Some linemen prefer to play with their hands rather than use the forearm as they attack the opponent. For this technique, the foot movement is exactly the same as described above. The heels of the hands drive *under* the shoulders of the offensive player. The hands, arms, and back lift the blocker's shoulders and force him back. This style of charge is difficult for tall men. It also presents the danger of the blocker getting under the hands to the body and the legs of the defender.

Using the Hands

Some defenders use their hands to ward off blockers (A). However, this runs the risk of the blocker getting under the hands to the body (B).

A   B

FIGHT THROUGH PRESSURE

One thing the defender must learn is that his most important reaction is to *fight through the pressure of the block.* As he feels which way the offensive man is trying to block him, he must fight that pressure. If he goes *around* the pressure, he will be taking himself out of the play, since he will now be behind the ball.

Offensive pressure

Always fight through pressure.   Never go around pressure.

OFFENSE

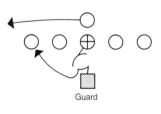

Guard

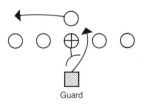

Guard

DEFENSE

PLAY OF THE NOSE GUARD

The nose guard is a down lineman who plays opposite—or "nose to nose" with—the offensive center. The basic assignment of the nose guard is to charge and defeat the center, never allowing the center to block him to either side. Some nose guards crowd the ball, which enables them to hit the center as soon as the ball moves. If the nose guard is bigger and stronger than the offensive center, then crowding the line of scrimmage is the most effective way to play. If the nose guard is not bigger and stronger than the center, he should drop back off the line of scrimmage about two feet. That will give him time to read

Position of the Nose Guard

Any nose guard bigger and stronger than the center should crowd the ball.

Any nose guard smaller and less strong than the center should play back off the line of scrimmage.

The nose guard (dark jersey) is in perfect position to fend off the center and move to the ball.

the movements of the offensive guards as he makes his charge against the center. To keep the center from blocking him to either side, the nose guard should step with his rear foot, bringing it about parallel with the forward foot as it was in his stance. He uses the hand-lift described above, raising the center up and forcing him back. By having his feet on line and his shoulders parallel to the line of scrimmage, he can successfully fight the pressure of the center's block to the left or the right.

In those alignments in which the down lineman is playing opposite the offensive tight end, his mission is to avoid being blocked inside by the end, but, equally important, he must also neutralize the end and keep him on the line of scrimmage. If the end cannot get off the line, he cannot be an effective pass receiver. Also, by controlling and containing the tight end, the defender keeps him from making a double-team block or getting across the line of scrimmage to block a linebacker.

The charge and play of the lineman against a tight end is exactly as described above to defeat a single opponent.

Theoretically, the defense will always have one free man, since only ten offensive players can block when one man has the ball. If a down lineman is able to occupy two offensive players, he will free an additional defensive man. By lining up on the outside shoulder of an opponent or in the gap between two men, the defender can charge either or both of them. And if he can manage to detain both at the line of scrimmage, another defensive man will be freed.

STUNT CHARGES

In addition to the basic charge of the down lineman, the defender must know how to execute other charges. If the offensive players are sure that all defensive linemen will simply charge straight ahead they can block more aggressively and effectively. But if they are not sure exactly how the defender will move, they must be more cautious in making their own charge. By using a variety of charges or "stunts," as they're called, the defensive man will confuse the blocking assignments of the offense. There are three basic stunt charges: *the slant, the loop,* and *the penetrating shoot-the-gap.*

Slant Charge

In a slant charge to the left, the defensive player steps with his right foot, aiming his forearm lift at the far shoulder of the offensive player. The second step with the left foot must get the defender past the blocker's head. He then makes his shoulders parallel to the line of scrimmage, finds the ball, and moves to it. The slant charge to the right is made in the same way, except that the first step is taken with the left foot.

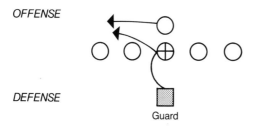

OFFENSE

DEFENSE

Guard

Slant charge to the left
The nose guard starts his slant charge to the left by making contact with the far shoulder of the center. He then turns so that his shoulders are parallel to the line of scrimmage and moves to the ball.

Loop Charge

The purpose of this charge is to get outside the offensive player. The defensive player starts by dropping off the line of scrimmage about 1½ feet. To loop to the left, the defender takes a lateral step with his left foot. Without advancing forward, he steps beyond his left foot with his right foot, being certain to get his right arm and shoulder past the head of the offensive player. He then steps again with the left foot, makes his shoulders parallel the line of scrimmage, finds the ball, and moves to it. The loop charge to the right is made in the same manner, except that the first step is taken with the right foot.

Loop Charge to the Left

A

B

The defender (light jersey) begins his loop left by taking a lateral step with his left foot (A). He then takes a long crossover step with his right foot (B), and with shoulders parallel to the line of scrimmage, moves toward the ball (C).

C

Shoot-the-Gap Charge Left

The defender penetrates the line by stepping into the gap at a 45-degree angle with his left foot (A). With his left shoulder and hip protecting against the block, he steps with his right foot (B). He is now through the gap and can move to the ball.

A

Shoot-the-Gap

When the offensive blockers are concerned about preventing the slant and loop charges, they become vulnerable to the quick-penetrating shoot-the-gap charge. To execute it to his left, the lineman steps quickly on a 45-degree angle to the inside, making penetration with his left foot. His left arm and shoulder shield his left hip and leg from the blocker. He then steps with his right foot to continue to penetrate. By stepping first with the left foot, he will make penetration and be able to place his right foot on the ground to withstand the pressure of the block from his outside. Having penetrated, the defensive player finds the ball and moves to it to make the tackle. To shoot the gap to the defender's right, the first step is taken with the right foot.

PASS-RUSH TECHNIQUES

On pass plays, the offensive blocker always tries to keep the opponent from penetrating through the line to the quarterback. When a defensive man makes a simple, straight-ahead charge, he will as often as not be stopped by the

B

offensive man, who can usually protect his area and keep the potential rusher from getting through to the quarterback. That may not be disasterous for the defensive man—if the play is a running play, he may still be able to fight through pressure and make a tackle. But when the defensive man realizes the play is a pass, he should use pass-rush techniques that will enable him to get *past* his opponent. The techniques are: *the swim, the cross-cut,* and *the wide loop.* Let's look at each.

The Swim

As the ball is snapped, the defensive man charges normally, since he is not sure whether the play will be a pass or a run. When he realizes the offensive man is passively protecting a zone to keep the defender from getting to the passer, the defensive man drives his fist and forearm up and over the shoulder of the blocker. When his arm, up to his armpit, is past the blocker, he uses his arm and shoulder muscles to pull down and raise his own body up and over the blocker's arm and body. Once past the blocker, he moves in on the quarterback. The arm movement is like that of a freestyle swimmer.

A

B

C

The Swim

In using the swim pass-rush technique, the defender (light jersey) first makes contact with the offensive blocker as he normally would—in this case using his hands (A). Once he sees that the play is a pass (B), the defender swings around his blocker (C), and throws his near arm over the blocker's head (D), almost as if he is executing a swimming stroke. He is now free to rush the passer (E).

D

E

The Cross-Cut

The arm movement in this charge, known as the "cross-cut," is opposite to that of the "swim." Again, the defensive man makes his normal charge, since he is not sure yet if the play is a pass or a run. When he realizes the blocker is protecting the passer, he drives his near arm and shoulder below his opponent's hands and past the blocking man's body. He then moves his arm and shoulder toward the line of scrimmage, pulling his opponent forward and freeing himself to move to the passer. Some teams refer to the cross-cut as the "down-under" pass rush technique.

C

A

B

The cross-cut (or down under)
As in the swim, once the defender (white jersey) sees that the play is a pass, he swings around his blocker (A). However, instead of throwing his near arm over the blocker, he drops his shoulder and slips his arm under the blocker's hands (B). He then drives his arm and shoulder forcefully upward until he is past the blocker and can move to the ball (C).

In "long yardage, sure-pass situations," two defensive players combine in a stunt called "the wide loop" to get penetration to the passer. The outside man drives inside the opponent in front of him with enough force to get penetration, even though the offensive guard sees him slanting to the inside and is prepared to block him. The inside defensive man steps toward his opponent with a normal charge to occupy him while his teammate is playing as described above. He then steps with his outside foot, crosses over with his inside foot and moves around the offensive tackle to penetrate to the passer.

The wide loop

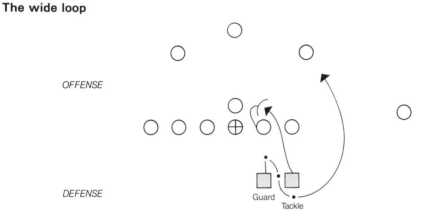

To summarize: The position taken by down linemen will vary depending on the defensive pattern being used. The linemen will line up on, or slightly off, the line of scrimmage, whether head-up with an opponent, shading to the outside or inside of an opponent, or in the gap between two offensive linemen. Regardless of the position, or the charge, the fundamentals of each play remain the same:

1. Take the alignment accurately.
2. Move with the snap of the ball and execute the basic charge.
3. Protect the designated area.
4. Locate the ball.
5. Pursue the ball on the proper angle.
6. Make the tackle.

Play of the Linebackers

Every defensive position is important, but the linebackers have the most difficult assignment on the defensive team because they must combine the skills of both the defensive linemen and the secondary men. They must be strong enough to defeat the blocks of the offensive linemen, quick and mobile enough to cover pass receivers, and intelligent enough to read their keys quickly and accurately. All in all, it requires splendid all-around athletic ability to play the position effectively. And to see it played by a Jack Lambert of the Pittsburgh Steelers or by a Rod Martin of the L. A. Raiders is to see it played to perfection.

STANCE

The linebacker's stance should be semi-erect. His feet should be spread approximately as wide as his shoulders, with one foot—preferably the outside foot—dropped back slightly. In his stance, the linebacker must have perfect balance so that he can move quickly in any direction.

Outstanding linebackers such as former All-Pro great
Jack Lambert possess consummate tackling ability.

The linebacker's semi-erect stance allows him maximum mobility in any direction.

KEYS

Usually the linebacker will key on an offensive lineman not covered by one of his own down linemen. The movement of that offensive lineman dictates the reaction of the linebacker. (See diagrams on pages 28 and 29.)

When the offensive lineman charges at him, the linebacker moves forward to attack, using his regular block-protection technique. When the lineman double-teams to either side, the linebacker should move forward quickly to penetrate. He should drive at a point just off the hip of the offensive blocker so that he will not be vulnerable to the trapping lineman moving from that side. When the uncovered lineman pulls to either side, the linebacker moves with him. When the lineman takes a drop step to execute a pass-protection block, the linebacker must drop quickly back to his assigned pass-defense zone. While dropping back, he must be alert to the possibility that the pass-protection block is merely a fake to set up the draw play. If it is, the linebacker must support quickly against the back who is running with the ball.

In each instance, after starting his reaction charge, which is dictated by the movement of the uncovered offensive lineman, the linebacker must find the ball, move to it, and make the tackle. When the play is a pass, he covers his zone or the assigned man until the ball is in the air, at which time he again moves quickly to the ball.

Keys of Linebackers

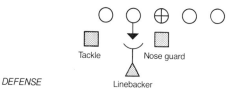

OFFENSE

The linebacker keys on an uncovered offensive lineman. If the lineman charges forward, the linebacker rushes forward to attack.

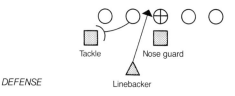

If the lineman doubleteams another defender, the linebacker penetrates.

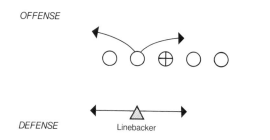

If the lineman moves to either side, the linebacker moves with him.

If the lineman drops back to make a pass-protection block, the linebacker should move to his pass-defense zone but be alert for the possible run.

STUNT CHARGES

To confuse the offensive blocking assignments, linebackers must on occasion move as the ball is snapped rather than wait to read their key before charging. The most common stunt charges are in coordination with a defensive lineman. If his teammate slants or loops to either side, the linebacker adjusts by moving in the opposite direction to cover the exposed area.

If the defensive plan is to have the linebacker penetrate to rush the passer or try to force the play for a loss, he moves opposite to *his teammate's* charge and penetrates across the line of scrimmage. He then finds the ball and moves to it.

PASS-DEFENSE RESPONSIBILITIES

The linebacker's ability to play effective pass defense is a fundamental ingredient in the success of his team. Generally, he will have two coordinated assignments against pass plays. First, he will always have a designated zone to cover on a pass. Second, while moving to the zone, he will be responsible for covering a backfield man who may run out to become a receiver. If his assigned back blocks, the linebacker continues to move to his designated pass-defense zone and plays the ball.

It is important that the linebacker get a fast key on pass plays. Most offensive teams will try to disguise their intention to pass, but the actions of the uncovered lineman in most instances will quickly indicate to the linebacker whether the play is a pass or a run.

The linebacker should always be concious that he must try to delay any eligible receivers who start downfield in his area. When the play begins, all of these men are potential blockers, and the rules allow the linebacker to hit them solidly with a block-protection-type blow. If the receiver is moving from the outside in, he remains a blocking threat and the linebacker can, within limits, continue to hit and delay him.

Perhaps the most difficult passes for the defensive team to cover are those that have a receiver crossing the field to the opposite side.

On plays of that type, the linebacker should imagine that he has to create a wall to prevent any outside receiver from crossing to the opposite side of the field.

As soon as they are in position to throw, most passers will look toward the area of the intended receiver. Passers are taught to avoid doing that, but

Linebacker Coverage on Pass Plays

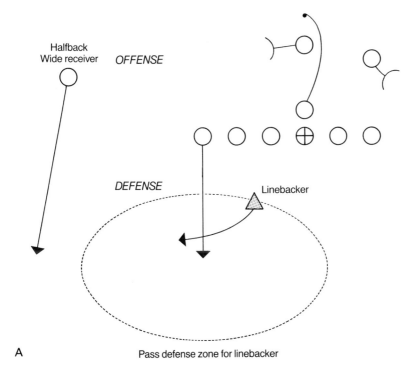

OFFENSE

Halfback
Wide receiver

DEFENSE   Linebacker

A

Pass defense zone for linebacker

On most pass plays, the linebacker covers a pass defense zone (A). However, when a backfield man runs out to become a receiver, the linebacker is responsible for leaving his zone and covering the back (B).

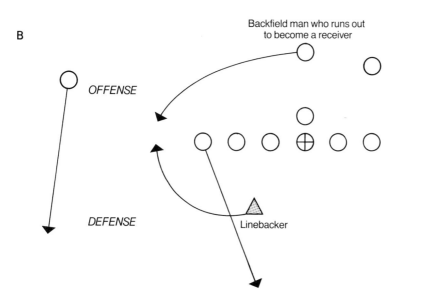

B

Backfield man who runs out
to become a receiver

OFFENSE

DEFENSE   Linebacker

only the highly skilled achieve such discipline in actual game competition. Thus, as the linebacker drops back, he should concentrate on watching the passer (always keeping in mind his responsibility to prevent an eligible receiver from crossing the field).

As the passer starts his throwing motion, the linebacker should immediately break in the direction the ball will be thrown. On drop-back passes, the linebacker should attempt to retreat quickly enough to reach the middle of his zone of protection before the ball is thrown. This spot is approximately 8 to 10 yards behind the line of scrimmage. If the linebacker does reach his spot of protection in time, he should bring his body totally under control and read the passer from a relatively motionless position. By setting up in that manner, he can make a more rapid lateral movement to the side the pass is thrown than he can if he is dropping back as the ball is delivered.

If the linebackers are quick enough to reach their zones and then make the described lateral movement as the ball is thrown, they will establish an effective wall that will require the quarterback to arch the ball over the linebackers to hit a receiver who is beyond 10 yards downfield. When the ball is

By moving back to their zone of protection, the linebackers force the passer to arch his pass over them.

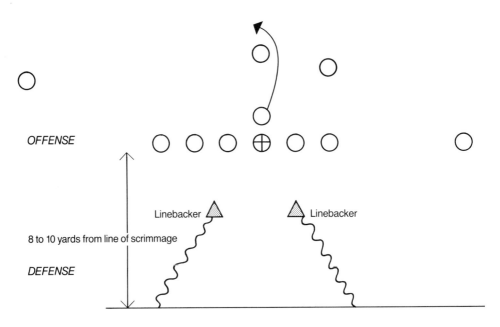

In this picture, both the line-backer (dark jersey) and the receiver (light jersey) are playing the ball legally.

Here the linebacker is playing the receiver illegally.

arched, it takes longer to reach the receivers than when it is "lined." This extra time will give the secondary men the opportunity to move to the ball before it reaches the target.

It is of fundamental importance that the linebackers—and all other defensive players—recognize that the rules give both teams an equal right to the ball the moment it is thrown. When the ball leaves the passer's hands, there is no offensive or defensive team, yet many defensive players subconsciously believe that the offense has a prior claim to the ball.

The rules prohibit defensive men from interfering with the receiver's opportunity to catch the ball. They also prohibit the offensive player from interfering with the right of the defense to make an interception. If either side is

Here, Lawrence Taylor of the Giants stays with a potential receiver. Note how Taylor's feet are set to move in any direction.

"playing the man," it is guilty of pass interference. If both sides are "playing the ball," they are both within the rules. Thus, when the ball is in the air, the linebackers must go for it with abandon.

On a passing play, the linebacker must both play his zone and watch for a delayed receiver coming out of the backfield. When this situation arises, the linebacker will be playing man-for-man defense. This assignment matches his speed against that of the offensive player—which again illustrates the rigorous physical requirements for linebackers. At the business of covering receivers, there are none better than Hugh Green of Tampa Bay and Lawrence Taylor of the Giants.

Playing the man-for-man defense is essentially a matter of moving on a proper angle of pursuit. A linebacker must move to the outside rapidly enough to prevent the offensive player from beating him to the outside. If the receiver attempts to break back to the inside, the rules allow the linebacker to maintain his position, and if he is in the right spot, he can legally hit the receiver and prevent him from breaking back to the inside of the field.

While moving on the proper angle to cover the potential receiver on the man-for-man assignment, the linebacker should have enough peripheral vision to be aware of the quarterback's movements. He should be especially alert to the moment when the quarterback throws the ball, and as soon as it is in the air, he should release his pursuit of the offensive man and move quickly to the ball.

It is an essential of team defense that all linebackers (and linemen) pursue the ball when it is in the air, regardless of their distance from it. If they stop their pursuit, they become mere spectators. The receiver may catch the ball, avoid the men in his immediate vicinity, and break away toward the goal line. If all defensive men are in pursuit, however, someone will usually be able to catch the receiver from behind, since his maneuvering takes time. Thus, defensive pursuit will prevent the touchdown.

Play of the Secondary Men

Defensive secondary men must possess all-around athletic ability. They must have speed enough to prevent the fastest man on the offensive team from getting behind them on pass plays. They must be tough, agile, and strong enough to tackle the shiftiest as well as the most powerful running backs. That calls for a combination of physical attributes.

Since football has become a two-platoon game, the skill of the offensive wide receivers has vastly improved. Offensive wide receivers possess track stars' speed. That requires that the secondary men have similar speed if they are to play effectively.

Today's wide receivers would have been virtually incapable of playing football back in the days when it was a one-platoon game. In one-platoon ball, the wide receiver had to play defense. But there is usually an inverse ratio between speed and physical toughness, and the lack of toughness prevents most men of great speed from playing well on defense.

An outstanding exception is Roy Green, of the Football Cardinals. In the NFL, he has been an outstanding defensive back and more recently has been selected by his peers as the number one wide receiver in the game.

67

On pass coverage, the best secondary men display speed, timing, and catlike reflexes.

STANCE

Regardless of the alignment being played by the secondary, the fundamental techniques for the cornerback or safety remain the same. His stance is similar to that of a linebacker. One foot should be dropped slightly back. The feet should be spread about the width of the shoulders, with the knees bent slightly. The arms hang loosely from the shoulders. From that stance, the defender will be able to move quickly in any direction.

The ready stance for a defensive secondary man

KEYS

All secondary defenders must think "pass" at the start of each play. They must defend against the possibility of a pass until they are *positive* the play will *not* be a pass. Only two developments after the ball is snapped can give them that certainty:

    1. An offensive lineman (tackle, guard, or center) crosses the line of scrimmage and moves downfield.

    2. The ball crosses the line of scrimmage.

    When either of those occurs, the secondary men may safely converge on the ball to stop the runner. But if they gamble that the play is a run and it turns out to be a play-action pass, the receiver may well get behind them for an easy touchdown.

In most defensive alignments, the secondary men can look through an uncovered offensive lineman to the ball. By keying on that lineman as the ball is snapped, they get a quick reading as to whether the play will be a pass or a run. This is the same reaction as was described for linebackers.

The paramount mission of the defensive secondary is to prevent the breakaway touchdown. Thus, secondary defenders must coordinate their movements, always keeping the ball in front of and inside of their unit until the tackle is made or the pass broken up.

There are two basic alignments for defensive secondaries: (1) four-deep and (2) the "monster" or rover-back pattern. In both alignments, the basic mission of the unit remains to keep the ball inside and in front until the tackle is made.

Secondaries play two types of pass defense, the zone and the man-for-man. In most situations, teams should use the zone pattern since it more effectively prevents breakaway plays.

Keys of the defensive secondary
In most cases, the defensive secondary keys on the uncovered offensive linemen.

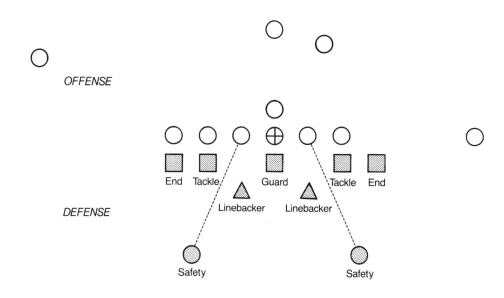

ZONE PASS DEFENSE

In the zone pattern, all men of the secondary drop back, keeping relative distances between themselves until the ball is thrown. Then they immediately move to the ball. They should read the passer's eyes and try to get the jump on the direction of the pass in the same manner described for linebackers.

If one member of the secondary drops deep while his teammate fails to drop back to the same depth, one deep zone will be left completely open.

When the team is playing the zone-type pass defense, the defensive linemen must rush the passer so that he will not have an extraordinarily long time to set up and throw. It is easy to maintain relative position in the secondary for five or six counts after the ball is snapped, but a longer time makes it difficult to hold the pattern and cover the receivers.

The zone pass defense

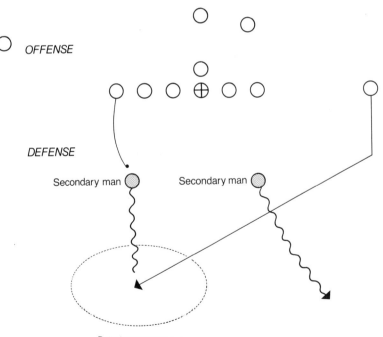

Dotted area indicates zone

When playing the man-for-man pass defense, each eligible receiver is assigned to a particular man in the defensive secondary.

In the man-for-man defense, a secondary man lines up relatively close to the line of scrimmage. He looks through his receiver to the ball, and when it is snapped he moves with the receiver, keeping him slightly to the inside and 1½ to 2 yards in front of himself. When the ball is thrown, the defender leaves his man and moves to the ball.

Occasionally it is necessary, and tactically sound, for the pass defense to switch secondary men after the ball is snapped. If the tight end breaks on a shallow course to the outside, while the wide receiver breaks on a shallow course to the inside, the coverage is easier if the cornerman and safety switch men and cover each other's receiver. Of course, practice and communication are vital.

Man-for-man pass defense

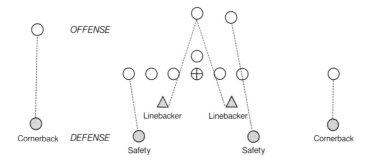

"Switching"
Defensive "switching" during man-for-man pass coverage occurs most often when receivers run crisscrossing patterns.

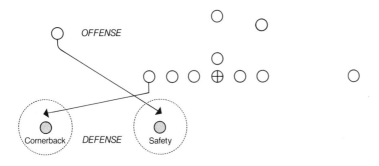

PLAY OF THE FOUR-DEEP SECONDARY

The four-deep secondary has two separate units—the cornerbacks and the safeties. One safety is designated as the "strong safety." He lines up opposite the offensive tight end. The other safety is called the "free safety." He takes his position to the side away from the tight end. The two cornermen line up 5 to 6 yards from the line of scrimmage, each opposite the wide receiver on his side.

On the four-deep-zone pass-defense pattern, the entire unit must move together and maintain relative position with each other as they react to the play:

The Four-Deep Defensive Secondary

1. When the ball moves to their left, the secondary men rotate in that direction.

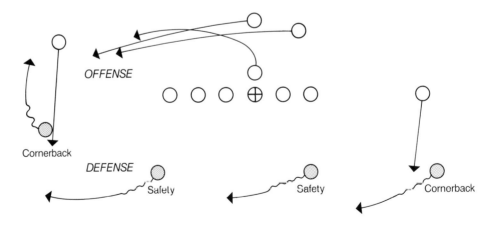

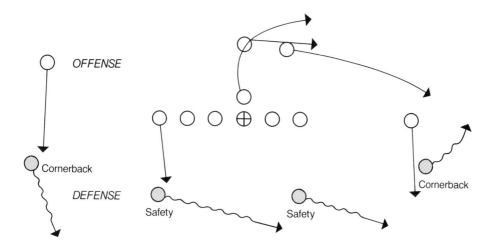

3. When the ball moves back, as the passer drops back to get in position to throw, the secondary men also drop back.

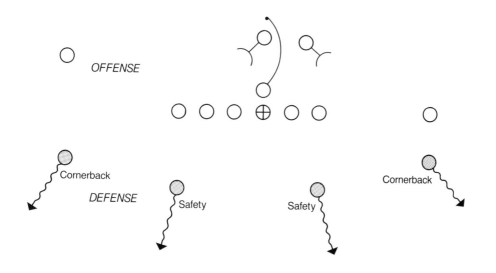

4. When the ball moves toward the line of scrimmage, as on a running play, the secondary men close on it.

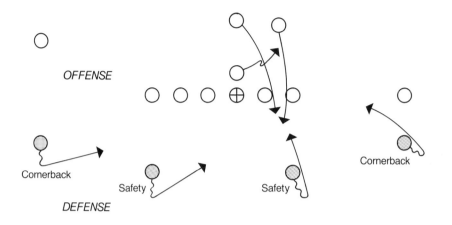

On all four basic movements, the secondary men must maintain their relative positions with regard to each other as they react to the situation.

Play of the Cornerbacks in the Four-Deep Secondary

When the ball moves to his side, the cornerback reacts as an outside linebacker would, by coming up quickly to turn the play in. When the ball moves in the opposite direction, the cornerback drops back quickly to be in position to cover his third of the field.

When the quarterback drops back to pass, the cornerback should also drop back quickly to cover his assigned pass-defense zone.

A dilemma for any cornerback is a play that begins as a run to his side but then develops into a pass. The running fake, which is directed at the cornerback, is the problem. To defend against this type of play, the cornerback should maintain a neutral position until the ball is approximately outside the offensive tackle.

When the ball passes that point to the outside, the cornerback must come up and force the play. If the passer sets up and prepares to throw inside of the imaginary line running behind the offensive tackle, then the cornerback must drop quickly back to cover his assigned outside pass-defense zone.

Cornerback Movement

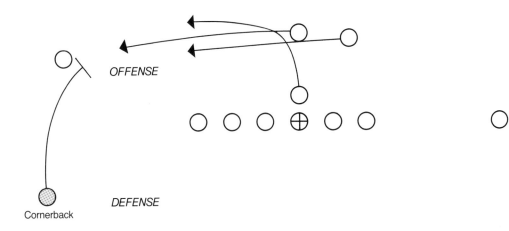

On a running play or screen pass to his side of the field, the cornerback moves in to help make the tackle.

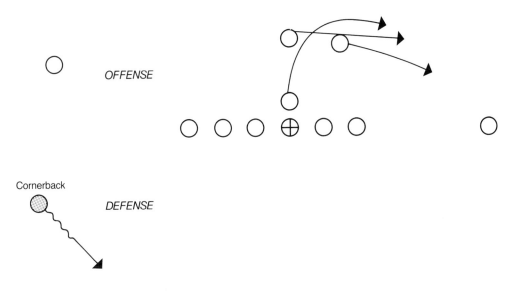

When the quarterback drops back to pass, the cornerback drops back into his zone.

Cornerback Play Against the Running Fake

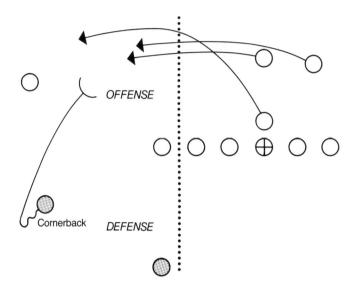

If the offense runs the ball past an imaginary line near its tackle, the cornerback runs in to force the play.

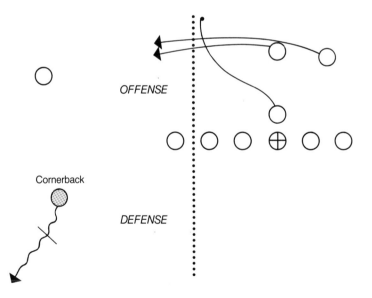

If the quarterback, before reaching the imaginary line, drops back to pass, the cornerback drops back quickly to cover his zone.

The offensive team will present a variety of formations to the cornerback. If the widest receiver is within 8 to 10 yards of the next widest receiver, it is possible for the cornerback to come up on plays in his direction. But if the widest eligible receiver is further to the outside, the cornerback must cover him deep, since the distance is too great for the safety to move over quickly enough to cover that receiver, who may run a deep outside pattern.

When the widest receiver is out so far that the safety cannot get over to cover him, the cornerback's assignment always remains the same: Cover the receiver deep.

Cornerback Coverage of a Wide Receiver

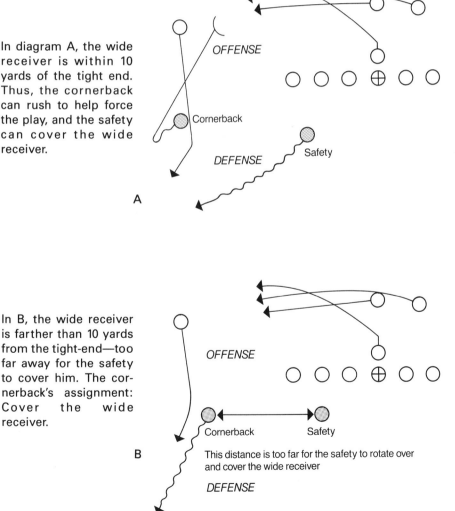

In diagram A, the wide receiver is within 10 yards of the tight end. Thus, the cornerback can rush to help force the play, and the safety can cover the wide receiver.

OFFENSE

Cornerback

DEFENSE   Safety

A

In B, the wide receiver is farther than 10 yards from the tight-end—too far away for the safety to cover him. The cornerback's assignment: Cover the wide receiver.

OFFENSE

Cornerback   Safety

B   This distance is too far for the safety to rotate over and cover the wide receiver

DEFENSE

The Bump-and-Run

A

The play starts with the cornerback (dark jersey) assuming the "ready" position 1½ yards from the wide receiver (A).

B

At the snap, the cornerback moves to the receiver, "bumps" him and tries to delay him (B).

Bump-and-Run Technique

Most receivers run excellent faking patterns, making it difficult for cornerbacks to cover them. To prevent the receivers from having room to maneuver to an open area downfield, cornerbacks can play the "bump-and-run" technique.

In professional football, men playing the "bump-and-run" cannot hit or obstruct the receiver after he has moved 4½ yards downfield. From the line of scrimmage to 4½ yards downfield, the defensive player is free to use his "bump-and-run" technique.

To play "bump-and-run," the defender lines up on the inside shoulder of the receiver about 1½ yards from him. As the ball is snapped, the defender steps into the receiver, hits him, and holds him up. When the receiver gets free (although a good hit might knock him off his feet), the defender turns and chases him. Obviously, the defender must be as fast as the receiver if he is to be able to keep him covered as he moves downfield. The defender watches the receiver as he chases him. When the receiver turns to look for the ball, the

C

D

If the receiver breaks free, the cornerback turns and chases him (C).

The cornerback concentrates on the receiver until the moment the receiver looks for the ball, whereupon the cornerback also turns and looks for the ball (D).

defender, too, looks back. Concentration is vital. When the ball is thrown to his man, the defender will be in the area, in position to break up the pass or to make an interception.

Play of the Safeties in the Four-Deep Secondary

The two inside defenders of a four-deep defense are known as the safeties. To simplify their assignments, they usually change positions depending on the strength of the offensive formation. Most offensive teams today use one tight end and one split end, who is a wide receiver. The safety who lines up to the side of the tight end is called the "strong" safety, while his colleague, who lines up on the side of the split end, is called the "free" safety because he has no immediate responsibility for any particular receiver coming deep. He is thus free to roam the secondary and give support where it is most needed.

The two safeties always react as a team. When the play moves to either side, they move to the outside in that direction.

Play of the Safeties in the Four-Deep Secondary

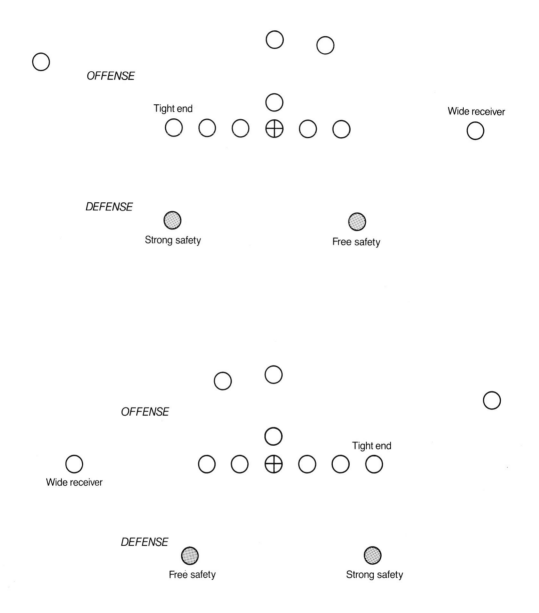

The strong safety lines up to the side of the tight end; the free safety lines up to the side of the wide receiver.

Teamwork Between Safeties

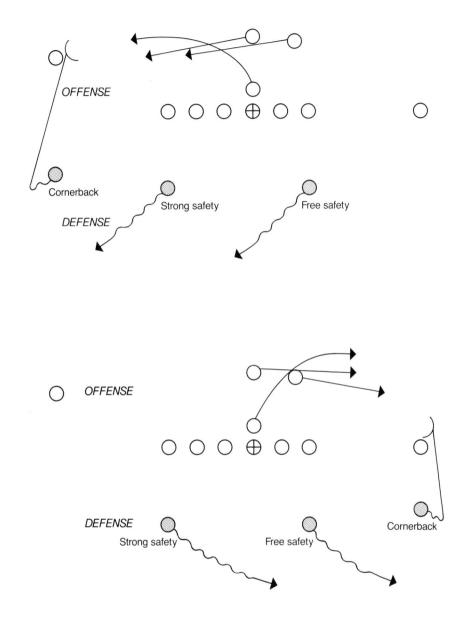

As these diagrams illustrate, safeties always work as a team.

As the cornerback comes up, the safety to the side of the play has deep outside responsibility, and the safety away from the play has responsibility for covering the deep middle zone.

On drop-back passes, both men move back to cover their assigned zones.

Safety movement on a drop-back pass

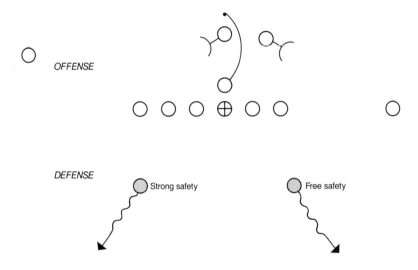

"Inverting"
The strong safety switches assignments with the cornerback and rushes in to force the play. The free safety covers the deep middle.

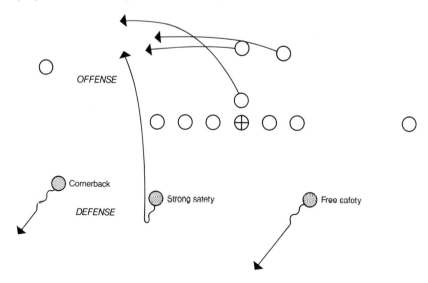

To change the pace and confuse the offensive blocking, the safety may, on a prearranged signal, change assignments with the cornerback. This adjustment is called "inverting." If the play starts to his side, the safety comes up immediately to force the play.

The cornerback now covers the deep outside, while the safety on the side away from the play moves in to cover the deep middle.

Both safeties must recognize the distance the wide receiver is split away from the next widest receiver. When this distance between the receivers is so great that the safety cannot get wide enough to cover the wide receiver on a deep outside pattern, the cornerback has the deep outside responsibility. Against such offensive formations, the safeties will play normally, or invert if the signal has been given to do so, at the snap of the ball.

PLAY OF THE "MONSTER" SECONDARY

The second pattern of secondary play is the "monster" defense. This pattern is used by college and high school teams to take advantage of the "wide field" when the ball is on the hash marks, and to exploit the skills of their personnel.

The monster defensive secondary
Note how much closer to the line the monster man (indicated by arrow) plays compared with the other secondary men.

The term "monster" varies at different schools to give color and elan to the position. At Michigan, the monster is called the "Wolf" man. At other schools, he is the "Husker," the "Bulldog," etc.

In college football, statistics reveal that the majority of long-gaining plays are run to the wide side of the field because of the additional room for the offense to operate. The monster defense responds to that threat by having an extra player on the wide side of the field. In practical terms, the defense is an overshift to the wide side.

Occasionally, as a change of pace, the monster alignment will overshift to the narrow side of the field to confuse the offense.

The monster pattern enables the defensive safety and the two defensive halfbacks to maintain their positions when plays move to the monster's side.

When the play moves away from the monster man, he moves back and in to become the middle safety. The safety and halfback to that side react as the safety and cornerback would on the four-deep defensive secondary.

When the play is a drop-back pass, the monster man can assist in double-covering any dangerous receiver in his area or else relieve the linebacker of the job of covering a backfield man who may come out as a receiver. The flexibility of the monster defense greatly reduces the pressure on the linebackers and the secondary, and this is the basic reason why the alignment has been used by so many college teams in recent years.

Every position on a football team is important, but the secondary is literally "the last line of defense."

Few football teams are capable of sustained offensive drives of more than 10 to 12 plays. They are penalized. Offensive assignments are missed, causing ballcarriers to be thrown for big losses. Fumbles occur.

The basic, cardinal rule of defensive secondary play is *always keep the ball inside and in front of the defensive secondary unit.* If that objective is achieved there will never be a long breakaway touchdown play, either by pass or run.

By never allowing a breakaway or even a gain of more than 15 yards on a single play, the secondary will force the offense to make a sustained drive to score. And since most offensive teams lack the consistency to sustain a drive of more than 10 to 12 plays, the defensive secondary gains a tremendous advantage in its unceasing effort to control the offense.

Defensive Secondary Movement

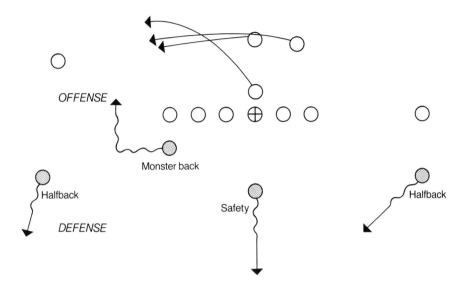

Movement of the defensive secondary when the play moves to the monster's side

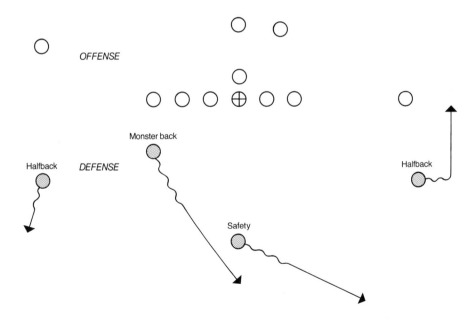

Movement of the defensive secondary when the play is away from the monster man

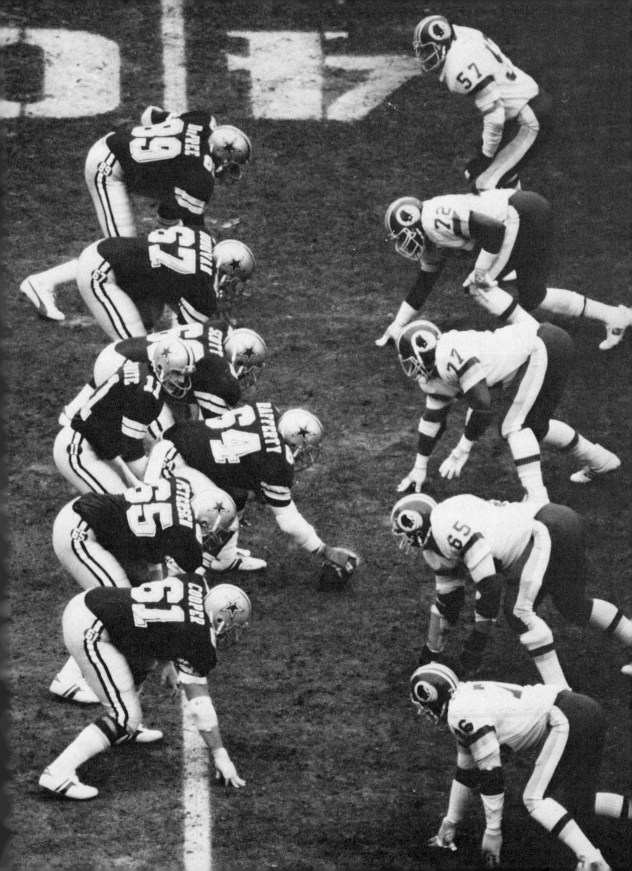

Defensive Alignments

In previous chapters, we have discussed some of the changes that have occurred in defensive alignments and patterns of play.

When football became a two-platoon game, it was found that players with the skills necessary to play *only* one offensive or defensive position could operate more effectively than men who had to play both ways. In addition, coaches switched from the single-wing formation to the "T" and began to use detached offensive players as wide receivers to force the defensive team to cover the entire field. That radically changed defensive strategy and tactics.

And yet . . . there is nothing new in football. Changes in strategy and tactics represent evolution—mutation—from older patterns of play.

Many coaches feel that my greatest contribution to defensive football was the development of what is commonly referred to as the "Okie defense." This defensive pattern has become one of the three commonly used alignments in today's game. But it was not a brilliant new idea. Rather, it was a mutation from an old defense used during the one-platoon days.

A basic defense in the 1930s and 1940s was the "7 box." The seven offensive linemen played

A defensive team's alignments reflect its overall strengths and weaknesses.

defense on the line of scrimmage. The fullback and a halfback played linebacker. The quarterback and the other halfback played safety.

The Okie defense was a logical adjustment from the 7 box to meet the strength of the commonly used offensive formations. The defensive ends dropped off the line of scrimmage and became cornerbacks. The five remaining linemen played on the line of scrimmage. The linebackers moved in slightly and played opposite the offensive guards. The two remaining defensive men became the strong and free safeties.

Basic Defensive Alignments

The 7 box defense
The "7 box" defense was popular in the days of one-platoon football.

The Okie defense
The author's own "Okie defense," a natural extension of the 7 box, was designed to meet the challenges of new offensive formations, particularly those that emphasized passing.

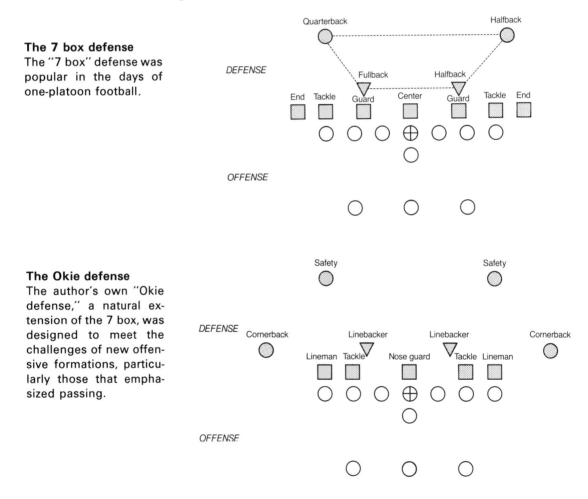

A team in that defensive alignment could adjust easily to the various positions of wide receivers and men in motion.

In today's game, there are two basic team defensive alignments; the four-deep and the "monster" alignment. The four-deep alignment always includes two cornerbacks, a strong safety, and a free safety. The remaining seven men use two different alignments—four down linemen with three linebackers, known as the 4–3, or three down linemen with four linebackers, the 3–4.

A team which has a greater number of capable linebackers than defensive linemen usually will use the 3–2 set. Conversely, if a team has a greater number of effective defensive linemen than linebackers, they will use the 4–1 set.

The four-deep alignment with the 4-1 interior set

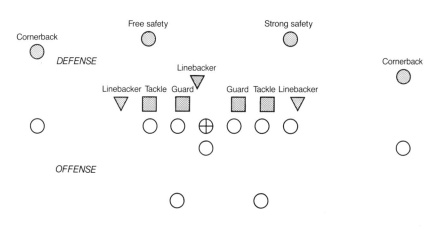

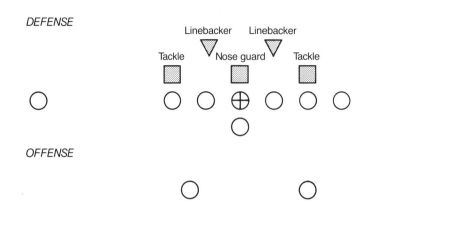

The 3-2 interior set of the four-deep defense

To simplify the four-deep alignment even further, think of it as always having two cornerbacks, a strong safety, a free safety, and two outside linebackers. The remaining five men are either in a 4–1 or a 3–2 set.

Applying this approach to the 3–4 alignment, we can say that the defense again has two cornerbacks, a free safety, a strong safety, and two outside linebackers, but the interior set now becomes a 3–2 instead of the 4–1.

The "monster" defense has one man, the monster, overshifted to the wide side of the field. The interior portion of the defense can be played as either a 4–1 set or a 3–2 set.

ADJUSTMENTS WITHIN THE 4–1 ALIGNMENT

Coaches are always trying to create a mismatch by having a stronger defensive man playing against a physically weaker offensive player.

In the regular 4–1 set, the defensive tackles play against the offensive tackles and the guards play opposite the offensive guards. In this alignment, physical mismatches usually do not occur. The outside linebacker plays over the tight end and usually they are evenly matched.

The Over-Alignment

To create a physical mismatch, defensive teams use what is called the "over-alignment." The adjustment is simple. The down linemen all move over one man to the side of the tight end. That puts a defensive tackle opposite the offensive tight end. The tackle, usually bigger and stronger than the tight end, should be able to defeat his block and should also be able to hold him up on probable passing downs. The outside linebacker to the side of the tight end now plays off the line of scrimmage and moves inside, setting up opposite the offensive guard. The middle linebacker moves one man away from the tight end, aligning himself opposite the offensive guard. The other outside linebacker moves up on the line of scrimmage where he can get an immediate penetrating rush into the offensive backfield. That alignment is almost exactly the same as the 3–2 interior set, but by having a big, strong defensive tackle opposite the tight end—instead of a linebacker—the defense has vastly improved its strength against running plays to the side of the tight end.

Over-alignment from the 4-1 defensive set

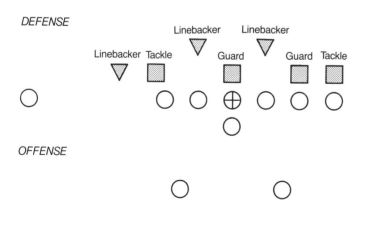

The Under-Alignment

When scouting reports indicate that the offensive team's running attack is particularly strong to the side of the split end, a sound defensive adjustment from the 4–1 is the "under-alignment." The four down linemen all move over one man away from the tight end. That change in alignment puts the defensive tackle on the side of the split end in position to get an unobstructed, immediate rush and penetration into the heart of the defensive backfield. The outside linebacker to the side of the tight end now plays exactly as he would in the normal 4–1 alignment. The middle linebacker moves out and plays over the offensive tackle to the side of the tight end, and the outside linebacker, who was to the side of the split end now moves in and plays opposite the offensive guard.

Again, the interior set looks almost like the 3–2 alignment, but the ability of the personnel—particularly of the defensive tackle to the side of the split end —to penetrate into the backfield usually results in a physical mismatch that makes it almost impossible for the offensive team to run effectively to the split end side.

Under-alignment from the 4-1 defensive set

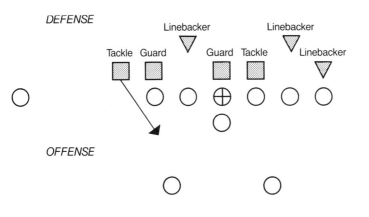

The 3–2 set is perfectly balanced and has men aligned to be able to match the physical skills of their offensive opponents. Each man on the line of scrimmage —including the outside linebacker who is playing on the tight end—must never allow himself to be blocked to the inside by his offensive counterpart. The same is true of the two inside linebackers: They must never allow the offensive guards to fire out and take them to the inside. If all those men do their jobs, then the nose guard is the only one who must protect both sides of his opponent, the offensive center. Since he usually has the physical ability to neutralize the offensive center, he can cover either side to stop the play. And with everyone else on the team protecting the outside, the defense can funnel all plays back to the inside.

As with the 4–1 defense, a coach can set up physical mismatches favorable to the defense by adjusting the interior alignment of the 3–2.

The basic 3-2 interior defensive set

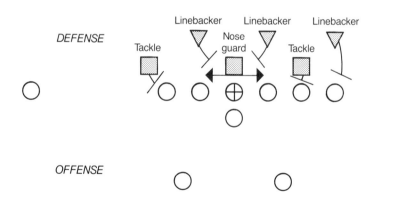

The Over-Alignment

On this set the nose guard and tackles move one man to the side of the tight end. That puts the defensive tackle over the tight end and creates a physical mismatch. The tight end is usually not able to block a strong defensive tackle. The outside linebacker, meanwhile, moves up on the line of scrimmage, from where he can penetrate immediately into the offensive backfield. The outside linebacker to the inside of the split end also is in position to get immediate penetration into the backfield. The two inside linebackers move one man away from the side of the tight end and now play opposite the offensive center and tackle. The alignment remains balanced, but physical mismatches have been set up and the ability of the two outside linebackers to penetrate immediately into the backfield adds to the defense.

Over-alignment from the 3-2 defensive set

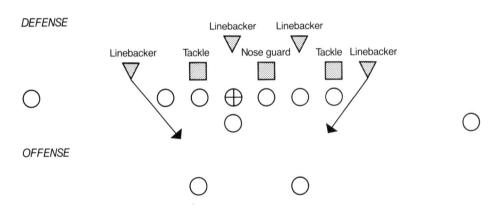

Stack Defense

The stack alignment is played to make it virtually impossible to run any inside play effectively. It also puts the linebackers in position to read the blocks of the offensive linemen and penetrate immediately across the line of scrimmage whenever the offensive tackle to the side of the tight end, or else the guard away from the tight end, blocks to the inside. Furthermore, the alignment allows three men—the two inside linebackers and the linebacker away from the tight end—to rush the passer when the ball is snapped. Such instant penetration by three men makes it almost impossible to run a play effectively inside and usually results in a successful rush of the passer.

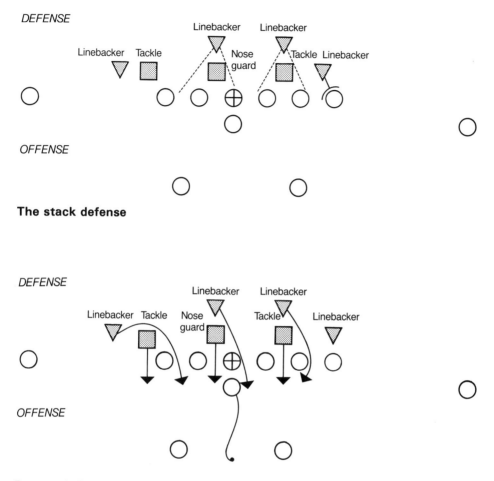

The stack defense

Pass rush from the stack defense

The alignment is played by moving the nose guard and tackles one-half man away from the side of the tight end. The linebacker on the tight end's side takes his position slightly inside of the tight end and makes certain that the end cannot get downfield to his inside—he must be forced to go outside or to try to block the linebacker in. The inside linebacker to the side of the tight end watches both the guard and the tackle. On a running play, he immediately shoots the gap to the side of the man who is blocking the defensive tackle. The same "read" is used by the other inside linebacker. He watches the offensive center and guard. He shoots the gap to the side of the block by the center or the offensive guard on the defensive nose guard.

From the stack, the effective pass rush has the nose guard and the tackles penetrating the gap in front of them. The outside linebacker to the side of the tight end rushes to the outside of the offensive tackle. The opposite inside linebacker rushes between the center and the offensive guard. The outside linebacker to the side of the split end rushes between the offensive guard and tackle. Since six men are rushing against five blocking linemen, someone should be able to get penetration immediately to put pressure on the passer.

The interior 4–1 set and the interior 3–2 set are balanced defenses. If the defensive players are as capable as the offensive blockers, both defenses are sound and will be effective.

Moreover, from both sets, the alignment variations described above can be used to set up physical mismatches. That not only confuses the offensive blocking assignments, but it also enables the defense to stop plays run at the strength of the adjusted alignments.

GOAL-LINE DEFENSE

When the offense has possession of the ball within five yards of the goal line, the goal-line defense is used and the designated personnel are substituted.

The most commonly used alignment is the 6–5, with six down linemen setting up on the line of scrimmage slightly to the inside of the offensive blockers. When the ball is snapped, they penetrate to their inside, attempting to get through every gap into the offensive backfield.

The remaining five men may be the regular four secondary men plus an inside or middle linebacker.

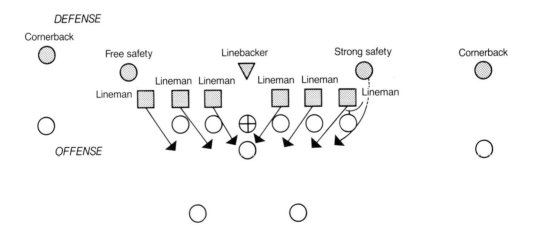

The Defensive Lineman's Goal-Line Stance and Charge

The defensive lineman's stance at the goal line (A) allows him to make a quick penetrating charge (B), shoot the gap, and gain penetration (C).

A

B

C

The cornerbacks cover the wide receivers to their side, but then are prepared to support quickly if their man attempts to block. The strong safety moves up and plays just outside the offensive tight end. If the tight end blocks the down lineman over him, the strong safety immediately penetrates and plays as a linebacker attempting to stop the running play if it comes to his side. The free safety also moves up. If the running play starts to his side, he will move wide of his outside defensive linemen to be certain that the running play cannot get around him. The middle linebacker assumes that there will be no effective hole to the inside. He is also ready to rush to the point of attack of any running play.

From a pass defense standpoint, the secondary men all play man-to-man. With the cornerbacks prepared to cover the wide receivers, the strong safety covers the tight end if he comes downfield to be a pass receiver and the inside linebacker and free safety cover any backfield man moving out as a pass receiver to their side.

Pass coverage in the goal-line defense

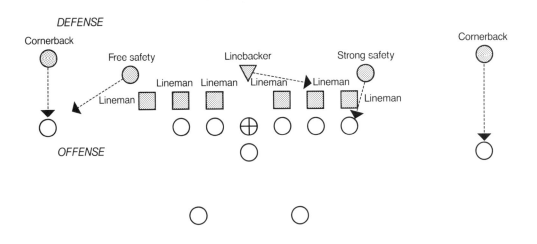

The goal-line defense is a gamble. The basic rule of the secondary—"keep the ball in front and inside"—is no longer applicable. The secondary must be ready to support quickly and take risks to prevent the offense from making any yardage. Any small gain in that area of the field can mean an instant touchdown.

It should be noted that some teams use a goal-line defense anywhere on the field of play when the offensive team has third down and short yardage— less than a yard and a half. But I feel that playing a goal-line defense far from the goal line is an unacceptable risk. Granted, the defense may stop the play cold and prevent the first down. If the offensive running play breaks past the line of scrimmage, however, a long gain or a touchdown often results, since there are no defensive men in position to pursue well and support the play. The same is true if the offensive team uses a pass play, usually a play-action pass. On man-to-man coverage, if any one man is defeated, a long gain or touchdown will result.

"PREVENT" DEFENSES

When the defensive team is ahead and time is running out in either the first half or the game, it is sensible to use what is known as a "prevent" defense, to ensure that the offense will not be able to break a play for long yardage. Occasionally, the "prevent" is also sound strategy on extreme long-yardage situations, regardless of the time remaining.

There are two standard "prevent" defenses: the 3–5–3 and the 4–5–2. Teams always substitute to have their most effective players in the game for either defense.

The 3–5–3 Prevent Defense

On the 3–5–3, three down linemen are used to rush the passer. The five linebackers may be defensive cornerbacks, safeties, or linebackers, but obviously, men possessing the greatest speed and reactions should be the ones to play those positions. They cover the five short zones. By dropping back as the ball is snapped, they give themselves sufficient room to move to the ball if it is thrown to a receiver in their zone.

The 3-5-3 Prevent Defense

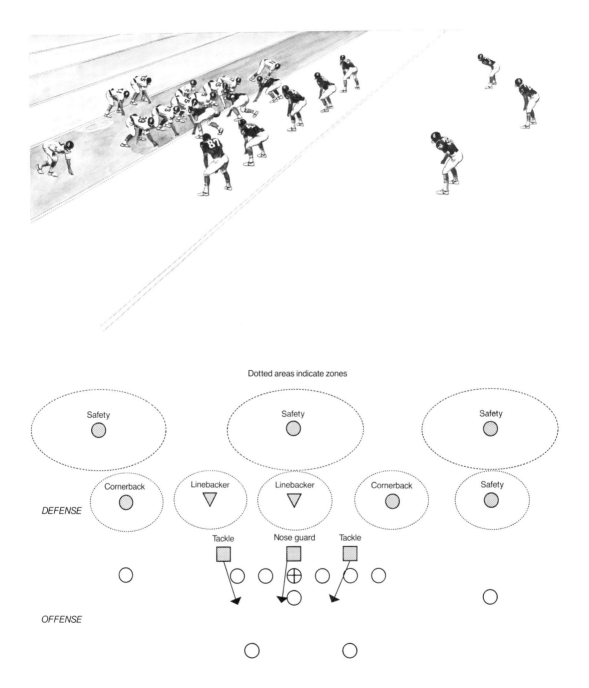

Dotted areas indicate zones

The three deep men are either cornerbacks or safeties. Their assignment is to cover the three deep zones. They are sufficiently far back from the quarterback that they have ample time, as the ball is thrown, to move to cover any receiver who is in their area.

The 4–5–2 Prevent Defense

In the 4–5–2 alignment, four linemen rush the passer. The extra man rushing should put more pressure on the quarterback than can be achieved from the 3–5–3 defense.

The five men playing as man-for-man pass defenders will usually be cornerbacks and safeties. The two cornerbacks cover the two wide receivers. The safety to the side of the tight end covers him. The two remaining short secondary men cover any offensive back moving out of the backfield to their side.

The two deep defensive halfbacks drop back deep and play the ball when it is thrown. They are also in position to support the man-for-man coverage of the short defenders.

The 4-5-2 Prevent Defense

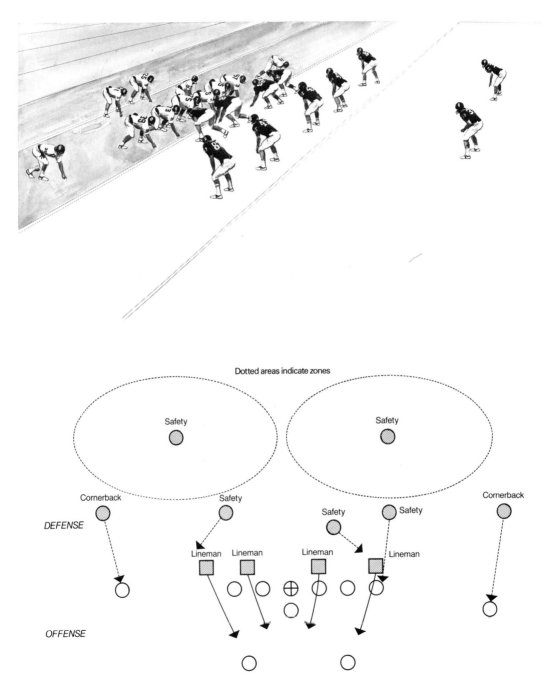

Dotted areas indicate zones

Safety

Safety

Cornerback   Safety   Safety   Safety   Cornerback

DEFENSE

Lineman   Lineman   Lineman   Lineman

OFFENSE

The "Nickel" and the "Dime"

Often, television or radio announcers will speak of the "nickel" or "dime" defense.

The "nickel" means that the defensive team has changed personnel within the 3–5–3 or the 4–5–2 to put more effective pass defenders into the game. The defense is used when the defenders are confident that the offensive team will throw the ball. The most common personnel change on the "nickel" is to replace the outside linebacker to the side of the tight end with a safety man, who represents the fifth secondary man in the game.

On the "dime" defense, *both* outside linebackers leave the game and are replaced by cornerbacks or safeties. That alignment has fully six pass defenders in the game.

Keep in mind, though, that there is never a guarantee that the offensive team will throw. Teams that go to the "nickel" or "dime" pattern no longer have their most effective personnel in the game against the running attack. If the offense does run, it could therefore be in a position to trample those men being used as special pass defenders.

If the offense must make more than 10 to 12 yards on one play to maintain possession of the ball, there is a minimal risk in using the nickel or dime, even if the offense runs the ball. If a six-yard gain will maintain position and a nickel or dime defense is used, the offense will probably be able to make first down on a run.

Needless to say, then, defensive coaches must carefully analyze the situation before they decide to use either of those prevent alignments.

The Defensive Kicking Game

Excellent execution of all phases of the defensive kicking game is a team fundamental that can lead to victory.

A truism is that the team with the most favorable vertical field position when the ball is exchanged will almost always win. Excluding interceptions and those fumbles that result in change of possession, all exchanges revolve around the kicking game. If an opponent never gets possession of the ball beyond its own 20 yard line, it is virtually impossible for that team to win.

For example, if on the first six changes of possession the opponents have the ball on their own 16, 25, 20, 22, 14, and 21 yard lines while our team gains possession on the exchange at our 45, the opponents' 40, our 48, our 42, our 40, and the opponents' 41, our team, says the truism, is almost sure to win.

Excellent execution of the defensive kicking game will result in favorable field position.

The kicking game is just as fundamental—and important—as any other phase of defense.

KICKOFFS

When it kicks off, the team's basic objective is to stop the opponents' return short of the 20 yard line. Obviously, that is most easily accomplished by having a kicker powerful enough to boot the ball through the end zone so that it cannot be returned. If the kickoff man lacks the leg-strength to kick the ball this far, he should practice kicking the ball as high as he can to give the covering team enough time to get downfield and make the tackle inside the 20.

In professional football, the kickoff team puts the ball in play from their own 35 yard line. College and high school teams, by the rules governing their play, kick from the 40.

Rule-makers believe the kickoff return is one of the most exciting plays in the game. Professional teams usually have a man who can kick the ball consistently about 65 yards. By having the kicking team begin the play from the 35 yard line, the rule-makers feel there is a greater chance that the receiving team will have an opportunity to return the kick instead of having it go into or through the end zone.

In recent years, college kicking specialists have been able to consistently kick the ball 65 yards or more. In an attempt to have the kickoff return remain a spectacular play, beginning with the 1984 season the college rule was changed. Now if the kickoff man kicks the ball beyond the end line, the receiving team will put the ball in play at the 30—instead of the 20—yard line.

While this rule change penalizes the most powerful kickers, it probably will result in more kickoffs actually being returned.

The kickoff team lines up, evenly spaced, across the field about 8 yards behind the line from which the ball will be kicked. The men who are to cover the kick must not cross their restraining line—the 35 in the pros, the 40 in college and high school—before the kicker has hit the ball. As the kicker starts forward, the men who are to cover the kick start forward with him but remain about 1 yard behind him until he has actually kicked the ball.

For coaching purposes, the men who will cover the kick are numbered across the field of play. The two fastest, most aggressive coverage men in the kickoff line should be the number 2 and number 10 players. It is their job to run downfield "with abandon," driving straight for the man who has received the kick. The other coverage men have lane assignments and stay in their lane to make sure the entire field is covered. They, too, run downfield as fast as possible. When they approach potential blockers on the receiving team, they should slow slightly and at the moment of contact get into the "hitting" position to shed or even avoid the blockers and continue on to the ballcarrier.

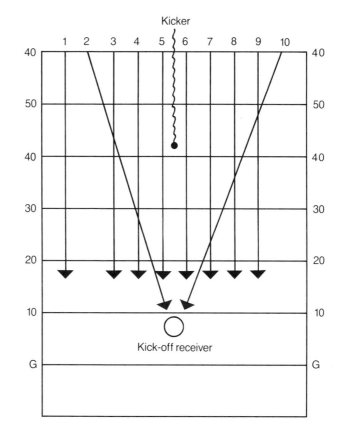

Defensive coverage on kickoffs
Players 2 and 10 move straight toward the kick receiver. Other players cover their "lanes."

It is a mistake if the men on the kicking team are about the same depth downfield as they cover the kick. Most of the time, this is not a problem since the men on the line possess varying speeds. Each man tries to cover as fast as he can, but since some men run faster than others, the varied depth needed as the line moves downfield is assured.

If all the men are of equal speed and run downfield in a straight line across the field, each man in his lane, the receiving team has only to break that one line of covering men to make a long return or a touchdown. By being at different depths the covering men can adjust their course to the ballcarrier's as they avoid the men attempting to block them.

The kicker is the safety man for the kicking team. He does not move downfield quickly. Rather, he aligns himself opposite the man who has caught the ball, watches the men on his team as they cover, and stays in position to make the tackle should the ballcarrier break past the first two walls of coverage.

Onside Kicks

When the kicking team is still losing after they have scored a touchdown or kicked a field goal, they may try to regain possession of the ball by making an onside kick.

The onside kick must travel 10 yards before it can be recovered by a member of the kicking team. Once the kickoff has gone 10 yards, it is a "free" ball and the team that recovers it gains possession.

Onside kicks are usually used late in the first half, when there is less time for damage if the onside kick fails, or late in the game, when it is a desperation gambit. It is simply bad strategy to gamble on the onside kick with lots of time remaining in the game since, by doing so, a team gives its opponent both time *and* favorable field position.

Occasionally, though, as a surprise, teams should consider beginning the game with an onside kick. It is almost sure to catch the opponents unprepared as they will be concentrating on executing their normal kickoff return rather than defending against the onside kick. The surprise value and the increased likelihood of success of the onside kick to open the game make it an acceptable gamble despite the loss of field position if the play fails.

Executing the Onside Kick

To execute the onside kick, when the kicker is ready to put the ball in play, the coverage men move across the field just before the ball is kicked, so that eight men are on one side of the kicker.

In moving toward the ball, the kicker disguises his intentions until the last moment, then squibs his kick *toward the sideline,* hoping he has given it just the right amount of bounce and spin so that it rolls no more than 10 yards

Movement of the defensive team for recovery of an onside kick

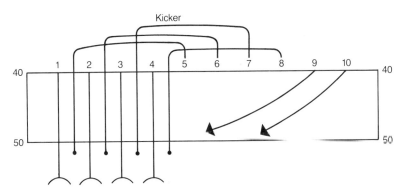

downfield. The first four men in the gang of eight ignore the ball and drive their immediate opponents back beyond the legal distance for recovery of the kick. The other four men, who are behind them, try to gain possession of the ball.

Usually the receiving team will adjust by moving their men across the field to counter those eight men covering as the ball is kicked. Occasionally, the kicker should kick away from the "loaded" side. When that is done, man number 10 blocks any receiver remaining on his side of the field and man number 11 attempts to recover the ball after it has gone 10 yards.

Penalties That Must Be Avoided by the Kicking Team

The most damaging penalty for the kicking team is to have a man "offsides" on the play. It is the result of overeagerness and lack of concentration on the part of the man who crosses the restraining line before the ball is kicked, and of bad coaching as well. There is simply no excuse for incurring this offsides penalty. Each man covering the kick should watch the kicker as he moves downfield. He should never cross the restraining line until he sees the kicker's foot hit the ball.

The major mistake that must be avoided on onside kicks is a man on the kicking team touching the ball before it has moved 10 yards downfield. If that occurs, the kick cannot legally be recovered by the kicking team—but the *receiving* team can choose to accept possession of the ball at the point where it was touched by the defensive man. Obviously, that results in outstanding field position for the receiving team.

DEFENDING THE PUNTING GAME

When the opponent goes into punt formation (usually on fourth down), the defensive team has two options: it can attempt to block the punt, or it can try to return the ball as far as possible.

All men rushing the punt must realize that the punter will move forward about three yards as he kicks the ball. The point they want to reach is 4½ yards *directly in front of where the punter takes his initial stance.* If the rushers do not aim for this point, they will not be in position to block the punt, and they run the additional risk of running into the punter, and incurring a 15-yard penalty for "roughing the kicker." That is one of the most disastrous penalties, since the 15 yards almost always result in a first down for the kicking team and enables them to maintain possession of the ball.

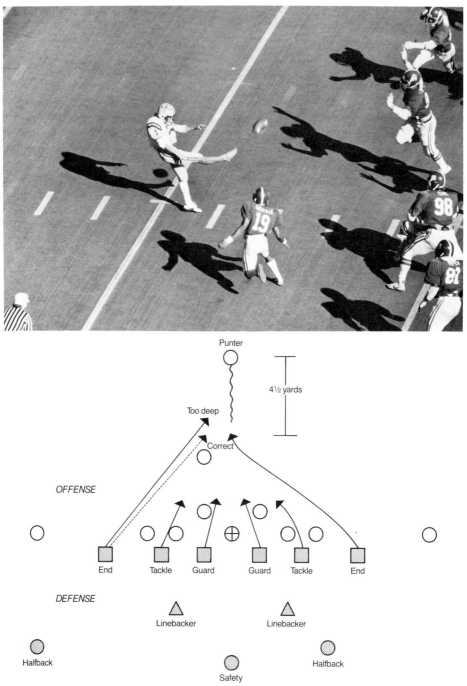

Punter

4 ½ yards

Too deep

Correct

OFFENSE

End Tackle Guard Guard Tackle End

DEFENSE

Linebacker Linebacker

Halfback Halfback

Safety

By rushing to a spot 4 ½ yards in front of where the punter takes the snap, a defenseman stands a better chance of blocking the punt without roughing the punter.

Blocking a Punt

The most common error made by men attempting to block a punt is to charge at the kicker. By doing that, they overlook the significant fact that the kicker will stride a step and a half forward and continue his forward motion as he drops the ball and prepares to kick it. By charging too deep at the kicker, the man attempting to block the punt will not put himself in the path of the flight of the ball as it is kicked.

Men attempting to block a punt should always aim for a spot 4½ yards in front of the kicker. By reaching that spot, they will be in the path of the flight of the ball as it is kicked and will be in position to block the punt.

Rarely does an interior lineman get penetration to that point, since the offensive team is always zone-blocking to prevent defensive players from getting through inside gaps. Nevertheless, the guards must charge aggressively through the gaps between the center and the upbacks, and the tackles must attempt to get penetration between the offensive guards and tackles.

The men in the best position to block the kick, however, are the defensive ends. They must run their course as quickly and aggressively as possible to penetrate to the spot 4½ yards in front of the punter and thereby be in position to block the kick.

Since the defensive team is never positive that the punter will actually kick the ball, the linebackers and defensive halfbacks usually watch the play develop instead of trying to assist in blocking the kick. By so doing, on a fake punt they are in position to cover any possible pass receivers or be in position to stop any running play.

The safety plays deep downfield in position to catch and return the punt.

When the defensive team decides to make an all-out attempt to block the kick, the linebackers move up and play on the line of scrimmage, and there is a furious, concentrated team effort.

The two defensive ends charge for a spot 4½ yards in front of the kicker. The defensive tackles shoot the gap between the center and "upback" to his side, occupying both offensive men. The right linebacker charges straight through the upback on his side, attempting to knock the blocker back. The right guard charges behind his linebacker through the open lane created and aims for a spot 4½ yards in front of the kicker.

The two defensive halfbacks watch the play develop and remain ready to defend against a possible pass or run. The safety plays deep downfield in position to catch the punt.

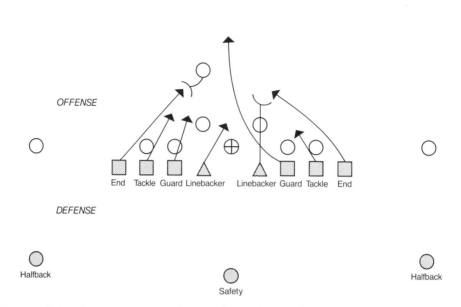

OFFENSE

End Tackle Guard Linebacker   Linebacker Guard Tackle End

DEFENSE

Halfback

Safety

Halfback

Proper defensive movement when rushing the punter

Punt Returns

Most of the time, if the center's snap is accurate and the punter's technique is sound, the punter will get his punt off before it can be blocked. From scouting reports the team should know its chances of actually blocking the kick. If the chances are not high, they should try to return the punt.

A well-executed punt return should always include a rush at the kicker. That puts those men rushing in position to block the kick if there is a bad snap from center (which delays the timing of the kick) or if the punter fumbles the ball.

The defensive linemen on the left side of the kicker try to rush the kick as hard and fast as possible. If they are not able to block the kick, they circle past the punter to become blockers on the return. While those men are rushing the kick, the linemen on the right side of the kicker step toward their opponent opposite them and use their hands, arms, and body to keep their opponents on the line of scrimmage so that they cannot get downfield quickly to cover the kick. They also force their opponents to make their getaway to the *inside* of the field. Then, men holding up their opponents move to the outside, parallel to the line of scrimmage. As soon as the return blockers reach a spot 12 yards from the sidelines, they turn downfield in the direction of the kick. Usually on this play the men trying to hold up their opponents move to the outside approximately three or four yards apart. They maintain this distance as they turn the corner and move downfield.

The men who tried to block the kick have penetrated across the line of scrimmage. If they have not blocked the kick, they, too, will be approximately four or five yards apart. They circle to the same point where their teammates turned downfield, which results in an evenly spaced wall of blockers approximately four or five yards apart moving downfield in a line and in position to block any of the men covering the kick. If the ballcarrier gets to their outside and they have not had an opponent to block, they reverse their field and run *with* the ballcarrier downfield again and are ready to block any man who comes at them from their inside.

Movement of the defense during sideline punt return by the defensive safety

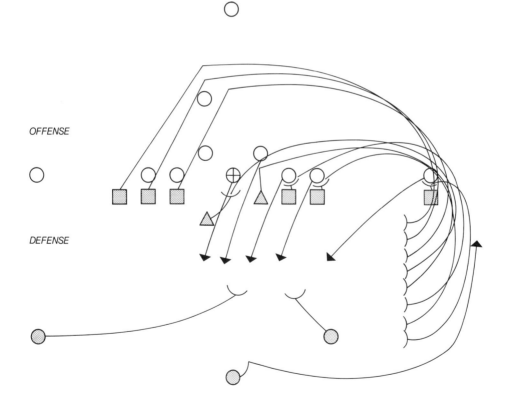

Only one man actually catches the punt. The three deep men who are in a position to handle the punt must always communicate quickly with each other. The ball usually comes to the middle man, but on occasion the punter may kick to one of the outside men. The middle man should shout, "I'll take it," or shout to one of his teammates, "Your ball." The two men who do not catch the punt move to spots five yards in front of and five yards to the side of the man who is making the catch. That puts them in position to block the first coverage man who gets near. Their objective is to give the man receiving the punt time to move to the outside of the wall of blockers.

If the receiver is able to get outside of the wall of blockers, he is probably assured of a long return or a touchdown, because the blockers should all have outside position on their opponents and should be able to knock them to the inside, giving the ballcarrier a clear lane for his return.

The Reverse Punt Return

When scouting reports reveal that the punter usually out-kicks the coverage men, the receiving team knows that it has time to execute the reverse punt return.

The play has the great advantage of keeping the men covering the kick from being certain which man on the return team will actually have the ball. That uncertainty delays their coverage. It also brings all of them to the inside, which makes it easier for the man who will eventually have the ball to run to the outside of the wall of blockers for a clear lane downfield.

If the reverse return is called to the receiving team's right and the man on the left side catches the ball, he fakes giving it to his teammate, keeps possession, and attempts to reach the wall of blockers.

Meanwhile, the blockers execute their assignments just as they did for the regular punt return.

As noted above, the deep men who are in position to catch the punt must always communicate quickly with each other as to who will actually catch the ball. The man making the catch must keep his eyes on the ball and move under it, and should *not* watch his opponents moving toward him.

When the opponents who are covering the kick are so close to the receiving man that they will be in position to hit him immediately after he catches the ball, the receiving man's teammates should shout, "Fair catch!" This will give the receiver time to signal for the fair catch, in which he trades the opportunity to advance the ball for assurance that he will not be hit by any opponent intent on forcing a fumble.

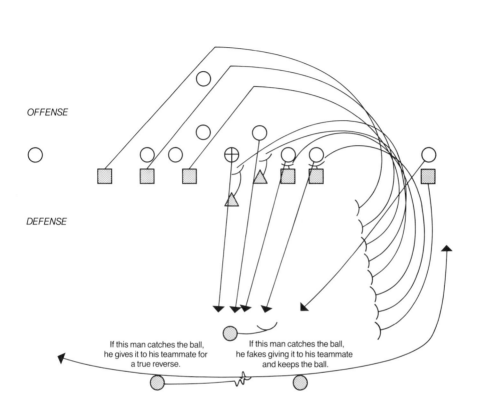

OFFENSE

DEFENSE

If this man catches the ball, he gives it to his teammate for a true reverse.

If this man catches the ball, he fakes giving it to his teammate and keeps the ball.

The reverse punt return

It is imperative that the man catching the punt *catch the ball on the fly and never allow it to hit the ground.* Most punters are able to kick the ball in the air about 35 yards beyond the line of scrimmage. When the ball is caught in the air, the kicking team will only gain the distance of the kick—about 35 yards. But if the ball is allowed to hit the ground and bounce forward 10 to 15 yards, as it usually does, the additional distance results in greatly improved field position for the kicking team.

When the kicking team puts the ball in play on or about the receiving team's 45 yard line, the men positioned to catch the ball know that the punter will either attempt to kick the ball out of bounds *inside* their 20 yard line or high and short so that it lands at about the 10 yard line. The men receiving the kick should catch the ball, either with a fair catch or an attempted return if the coverage men are slow, if the ball comes down outside the 5 yard line. If the ball will land deeper than their 5 yard line, they should not touch the kick. Rather, they should let it hit the ground and hope it will bounce into the end for a touchback.

In every situation then, the defensive punting game must be well executed to give the receiving team their most advantageous point of possession on the exchange.

Punt Defense When the Kicking Team May Not Kick but Instead Run or Pass

When the offensive team goes into punt formation, the defense can never be certain that they will actually kick the ball. The offense may decide to use a running play or throw a pass.

The likelihood of a fake depends on the score, the time remaining, and the vertical field position of the ball. Whenever the offensive team goes into a punt formation on the defensive team's 45 to 35 yard line—just beyond field goal range—the defense should be particularly alert and ready to stop a running or pass play.

Whenever the defensive team is not reasonably sure the offensive team will actually punt, they must be prepared to play a sound defense against the pass or run instead of putting maximum pressure on the kicking team to block the kick.

As the ball is snapped, the two defensive ends come straight across the line of scrimmage and play in position to prevent any ballcarrier from getting to their outside. The defensive tackles shoot the gap between the offensive guards and tackles. The guards charge at the two upbacks.

Those charges put all men in position to adjust to any play being run, and by getting good penetration on the angles described, they are in reasonable position to continue to rush the kicker.

The two linebackers and the two defensive halfbacks use their normal reactions to stop a run or a pass if the kicker does not actually punt the ball.

The defensive safety plays deep downfield in position to catch the punt if the ball is kicked.

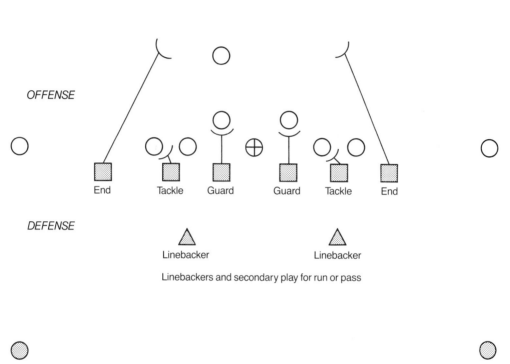

OFFENSE

End   Tackle   Guard   Guard   Tackle   End

DEFENSE

Linebacker   Linebacker

Linebackers and secondary play for run or pass

Halfback   Halfback

Safety

Punt defense when the kicking team may not punt but instead run or pass

FIELD GOALS

When the kicking team lines up in a field-goal formation, there is no certainty that it will actually kick the ball. It might run or throw from the field-goal set. The defending team, therefore, while fundamentally trying to block the kick, must always be prepared to stop a pass or a run.

Basic Defensive Alignment

Substitutions are made so that the field-goal defensive team is composed of the most capable players available.

The linemen who are used should be the quickest, strongest men on the team. They take their position on the line of scrimmage and shoot the gap in

Basic field-goal defense

front of them, attempting to get penetration to a spot 3½ yards in front of the
ball.

If the ball is not kicked, they react to the pattern of the play being run, adjusting their course to tackle the ballcarrier or rush the passer.

Each of the two defensive halfbacks keys the tight end and wingback on his side. If either of those men does not block, but instead comes downfield as a possible pass receiver, the defensive halfback must cover him.

The safety adjusts his depth from the line of scrimmage to the distance the kicker is from the goal line. If the safety is sure the kicker is strong enough to kick the ball beyond the endline, he should line up 5 to 8 yards behind the line of scrimmage in position for a fake. He will move forward to stop a running play, or back to defend the deep middle zone on a pass.

When the kicker is attempting a long field goal—more than 40 yards from the goalposts—the safety should line up about 20 yards from the line of scrimmage in position to field the kick if it falls short and can be returned.

Blocking a Field Goal or Extra Point

To block a place kick, the defensive team should substitute men who have the best skills needed to execute the play.

The kicking team will always be in the same formation. They have the center and six offensive linemen on the line of scrimmage, with no space between them. The other two blockers set up as wingbacks. The holder is 7 yards from the line of scrimmage. The kicker is a step and a half behind the holder.

When the ball is snapped, the offensive players form a solid wall in an attempt to prevent any defensive man from getting penetration to the flight of the ball as it is kicked. The center snaps the ball and holds his ground. The other linemen drop step with their outside foot. They attempt to keep any man from penetrating through the gaps to their inside. The two wingbacks step up with their inside foot and attempt to make a solid wall between themselves and the offensive ends.

How do the defenders counter?

The middle defensive guard charges the center as hard as possible, in an effort to disrupt his ability to snap the ball and then, if possible, to drive him back.

The other two defensive guards charge through the gap between the offensive guard and tackle on their side of the center.

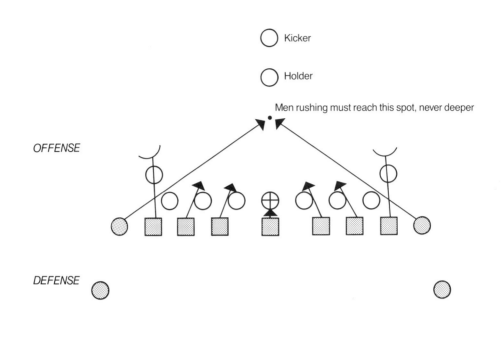

Kicker

Holder

Men rushing must reach this spot, never deeper

OFFENSE

DEFENSE

Defensive movement for blocking a field goal

The defensive tackles charge through the gap between the offensive tackles and ends.

The two defensive ends charge at the inside shoulder of the offensive wingbacks. They attempt to knock them back and to the outside. These charges should open gaps between the offensive ends and wingbacks.

That enables defensive halfbacks to shoot the gap between the wingbacks and offensive ends. The two halfbacks penetrate through those gaps to the path of the flight of the ball. The spot for which they aim is 2 yards in front of the holder. They are the men likeliest to block the kick.

The other two defensive halfbacks watch the play develop and stay in position to adjust to a possible bad snap from center that might result in a run to their side by either the holder or kicker.

In college football and the USFL, the team that scores the touchdown has the option of kicking the ball to make one point or using a run or pass play to take the ball the three yards to the end zone for two points. In the NFL, teams must settle for the one-point conversion. I believe it would improve the NFL game if their rule were changed to include the option of going for one or two points.

After a touchdown, when the kicking team lines up in a field-goal formation, the defenders should use the "block kick" play described above because the offense almost certainly will kick the ball. But if the offensive team lines up in a normal formation and the quarterback is set to receive the snap from center in his regular position, or from the "shotgun" set, the other team must immediately substitute its regular goal-line defensive team.

On a two-point conversion attempt, about 90 percent of the time the offensive team will use a "pass-run" option play, throwing the ball if a receiver is open or running it if the receivers are covered.

The goal-line defense should operate exactly as described for the regular goal-line defense, but every man on the team should be alert for the most likely play, the "pass-run" option.

Defensive Strategy

To play effective defense, a team must have the proper mental attitude. Instead of being concerned with merely stopping their opponent, they must attack the offensive team on every play. By attacking the opponent—that is, trying to shut them down for no gain or even a loss—they force the offensive team into worrying about what they, the defense, will do next. That changes the mental balance of the game. The confidence of the offensive team begins to break down. They start making mistakes. And before long they are unable to execute their offensive plays with any kind of precision.

Effective defensive football has a direct relationship to the vertical field position of the ball. When the opponents have the ball outside the defender's 35 yard line, they have only three downs to make a first down, since they must kick the ball on the fourth down or risk surrendering it at that spot. Inside the defenders' 35, the offense has the luxury of a fourth attempt in each series, since if they are stopped short of a first down they are still giving their defensive team favorable field position. Inside the 35 the offense also may be in position to try for a field goal on fourth down.

123

The harder a defense attacks, the more likely it is that the opponent's game plan will break down.

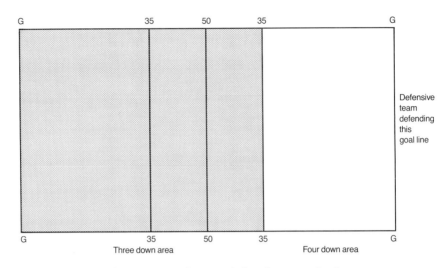

```
G              35      50      35              G
                                              Defensive
                                              team
                                              defending
                                              this
                                              goal line

G              35      50      35              G
        Three down area        Four down area
```

Three-down and four-down areas from a defensive standpoint

IMPORTANCE OF POINT OF EXCHANGE

In planning the tactics and strategy to win a football game, the "point of exchange" is one of the two most important factors. (The other important factor is "time of possession." The team that has possession of the ball the majority of the time usually wins. For example, if our team has the ball for 40 minutes, and the opponents for only 20, our team should win.)

The point of exchange refers to the spot on the field where the offense surrenders the ball to the opponent. The team that has the most favorable field position, cumulatively, on the exchanges will almost always win the game.

Favorable field position on the exchanges is the result of a strong kicking game, a consistent offense, the avoidance of turnovers, and a solid defense.

The strong kicking game combines the ability to kick the ball out of the end zone on kickoffs, or to kick it high enough and cover so quickly that the opponent is stopped on the return inside of his own 20 to 25 yard line. When forced to punt, it is the ability to make 35 net yards on the play. That requires a punter who can kick well and team speed in covering the kick.

A consistent offense implies the ability to make at least two or three first downs each time a team gains possession of the ball.

The third factor in gaining and maintaining favorable field position is the avoidance of the two major errors of fumbles and pass interceptions. Each time either occurs, generally speaking, the offensive team has surrendered a minimum of the 35 yards it could have made had it punted on the play.

Assuming that the ball is in possession of the offensive team in its own territory—the three-down area—the defense has the problem of keeping the offense from averaging 3⅓ yards per play. If the offense makes that much yardage on each of the three plays, it will have made a first down. When the ball is in the four-down area of the field, the offense need only average 2½ yards per play.

CREATING OFFENSIVE ERRORS

Assuming sound, consistent execution on the part of the offense, the percentages are in its favor if it avoids errors such as fumbles, interceptions, penalties, and assignment mistakes. Most offensive teams can avoid those errors for a limited number of snaps. But the more times it must put the ball in play to score, the greater the odds are that the offense will commit an error. A successful offensive play requires the coordinated execution of eleven men, and that is a difficult feat to achieve for more than ten or eleven consecutive snaps.

By attacking the offensive team and using a variety of alignments and defensive stunts, the defenders will be able to force a "bad" play—a play that loses yardage and creates a long-yardage situation.

It should be noted that something like 75 percent of penalties going against the offense again result in long-yardage situations.

NECESSITY OF AVOIDING BREAKAWAY PLAYS

The difficulty of avoiding errors on offense is the prime reason why the point of exchange is so vitally important in the ultimate outcome. If the opponent always gets the ball a long way from the defenders' goal, and if the defenders play soundly by avoiding long gaining plays, the defense will be able to force an error on the part of the offense. That will result in an unfavorable down-and-yardage situation for the offensive team.

It is comparatively easy for the offense to make 3⅓ yards on any one play. But, if the offense can be forced into a situation where it must make six yards or more on a succession of plays to make the first down, the advantage passes to the defense. Thus, a prime objective of the defense must be to create a long-yardage situation. There is, however, one prior objective—the avoidance of a breakaway play.

A breakaway play may be defined as one that gains 20 yards or goes all the way for a touchdown. Gains of that length can be avoided if the defensive

Breakaway plays result from bad tackles by defensive linemen or from errors in coverage by the defensive secondary.

secondary plays correctly and always keeps the ball in front of and inside of its unit. A ball thrown 20 yards or more down the field is in the air long enough for the secondary to get to it and break it up if the members are reading their pass keys properly.

Breakaway plays result from errors by the secondary. If that unit executes its basic objective and gets reasonable support from the linemen and linebackers, no breakaway plays can be made.

HOW TO CREATE A LONG-YARDAGE SITUATION

With the secondary playing error-free football, it now becomes the mission of the linemen and linebackers to create a long-yardage situation by any of the following means:

1. A penalty against the offensive team
2. An offensive ball-handling error resulting in a loss on the play
3. An offensive assignment error enabling the defensive player to make the tackle behind the line of scrimmage
4. A well-executed defensive maneuver by the linemen and linebackers resulting in a loss of yardage on the play

It may appear to be negative thinking to assume that the opponent will be penalized so that the defensive team is treated to a long-yardage situation. But it remains a fact that the vast majority of offensive teams will incur a penalty if they are required to put the ball in play 15 or 20 consecutive times. Some offensive player will hold, jump offside, clip, botch the formation. Thus, a defensive team that plays sound field-position football can, except against a truly excellent opponent, expect to get a long-yardage situation as a result of a penalty if the team combines perfect defense against breakaway plays with excellent field position at the point of exchange.

The same is true of backfield ball-handling errors. While offensive teams are expected to handle the ball flawlessly, the fact remains that if they are required to put the ball in play a number of times in succession, sooner or later someone will mishandle it. And even though the offense may recover its fumble, yardage will more than likely be lost on the play and a long-yardage situation will be created.

All offensive linemen have blocking rules that, if properly followed, will have each man taking out an assigned defender. Again, while mistakes should not occur, the defense can sooner or later expect to force an offensive error if it plays intelligently and varies its alignments. Then the defenders will move in, throw the ballcarrier for a loss, and once again create their coveted long-yardage situation.

TEAM STUNTS

The preceding three means of creating a long-yardage situation require the cooperation of the offensive team. Excellent opponents—and there are few of those in actual competition—will not make those self-defeating errors. Against such good teams, to deny the offense the 3⅓-yards-per-play average, it will be necessary for the defense to employ a stunt that will enable it to penetrate behind the line of scrimmage and throw the ballcarrier for a loss. Such stunts are relatively simple to execute and are a combination of a slant or loop charge by a lineman or end and a "read-key" by the linebacker. (See page 27).

There are almost unlimited numbers of ways these combinations of line charges and keying by linebackers put pressure on the offense.

Slant Charge to the Right

For example, the linemen can start a charge by slanting to their right. The left end must step with his right foot and hold up the offensive tight end so that he cannot block a linebacker. If the ball moves to the right, the right-side linebacker will shoot the gap between the guard and the tackle. Four men are now penetrating if the play goes that way, and a loss is almost sure to result. The left-side linebacker, by reading his key (the side to which the ball is going), simply moves to his right and plays as a regular linebacker.

If the play goes away from the slanting linemen, the defense is still sound. The linemen are slanting to the right, but the play goes to their left. That changes the key of the linebackers. When the ball moves to the left, the left-side linebacker shoots the gap just outside the offensive tackle. That charge, coupled with the slant of the linemen on the tackle, has two men penetrating on the side where the ball is. The right linebacker, also by reading the key, moves to his left to support normally.

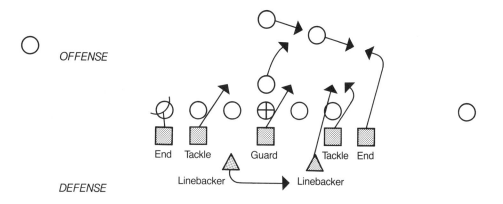

Defensive lineman slant to their right, offense runs play to the defense's right

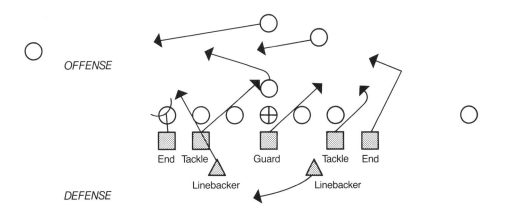

Defensive linemen slant to their right, offense runs play to defense's left

Slant Charge to the Left

Let's say, though, that the linemen slant to the *left,* and the ball moves to the left. The linebackers use the same keys described above. The left linebacker shoots the gap between the guard and tackle, giving four-man penetration on that side. The right linebacker reacts normally, moving to his left. Sometimes, of course, the linemen may slant to the left and the ball moves to the right. But by shooting the gap outside the offensive tackle, the right linebacker may get through. The left linebacker supports normally.

By using defensive stunts of that kind, particularly when a running play is expected, it is possible to break into the backfield and stop the ballcarrier for a loss. Such maneuvers weaken the pass defense, but the unexpected rush of the linebackers may enable a defensive player to get to the passer before he can throw and thus again create the long-yardage situation.

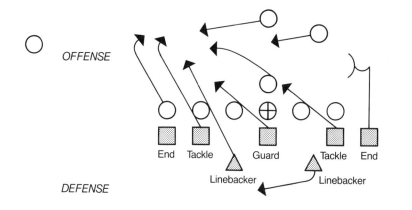

Defensive linemen slant left, offense runs play to defense's left

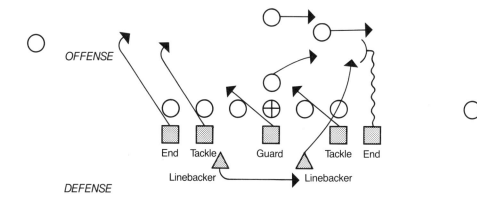

Defensive linemen slant left, offense runs play to defense's right

The best defensive squads seem to swarm to the ball on every play.

On every play, all defensive men must be conscious of the "down-and-distance" situation. That means they must be aware of the yardage needed by the offensive team to make a first down and thereby retain possession of the ball.

Once a long-yardage situation has been achieved, the objectives of the defense change. When a second-down-and-15-yards-to-gain situation has been created, the defense can allow the offense to make seven yards on the next two plays (if it is in the three-down area of the field) and still force it to surrender the ball.

In such situations, the defense should not attempt to *force* the play with so much vigor that it loses the swarming effect of every man being part of the pursuit pattern. The defensive players should all think: "We can let them make five or six yards on this play and still be in control of the situation." The mental adjustment will make it extremely difficult for the offense to make the first down.

By following the sound defensive plan outlined above, waiting for an offensive error, and limiting the offense to relatively short gains, the percentages will favor the defensive team.

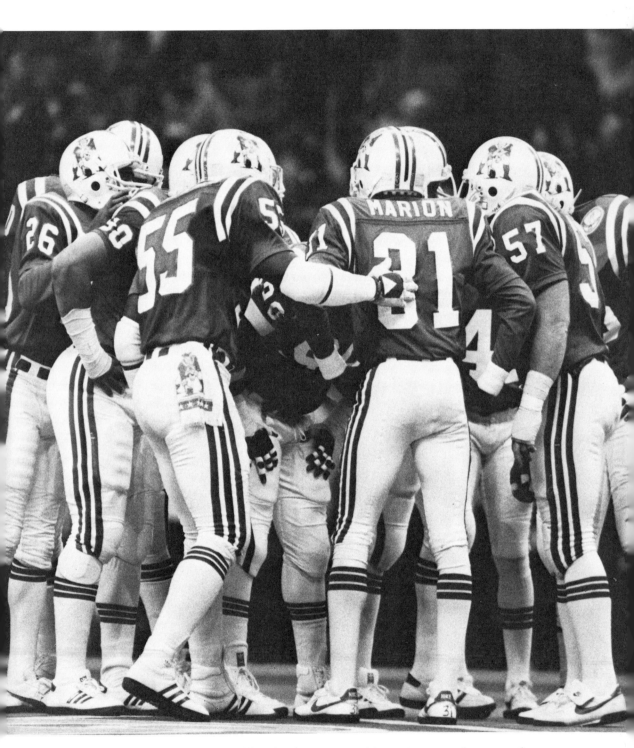

"Defensive signal-calling is always something of a guessing game."

Coordinated Defensive Plan

All football followers recognize that offensive teams use a variety of formations. From each formation they have a complete offense, which enables them to call straight-ahead running plays, counters, reverses, and all types of passes. The defensive team must also have a variety of plays with which to attack the offense, regardless of the formation the offense is in.

The defense begins its strategy from its chosen basic alignment—the most common, as we have seen, being the 4–1 interior set or the 3–2 set.

The defensive "quarterback" is the man who calls the defensive signals. He is usually a linebacker. Rarely in today's game does he actually select the defense to be used. Instead, he looks to the sidelines where a coach will signal to him the defensive play he should call. In most cases in collegiate or professional competition, the coach who signals in the defensive play has been instructed on the call from a coach in the press box, who has a much better view of the entire field.

To be certain the entire defensive team on the field gets the correct signal, it huddles about a yard and a half behind the line of scrimmage. There they can hear the signal called by the defensive quarterback and be in a position to break the huddle quickly should the offensive team (which, remember, controls *when* the ball is put into play) line up and snap the ball much more quickly than usual, in an attempt to catch the defense before they can properly line up.

Defensive signal-calling is always something of a guessing game. The defensive coaches have carefully studied their scouting reports and the "tendencies" of the offensive team. The factors they consider are remarkably varied. What does the offense usually do on first and 10—run or throw? What run are they most likely to use? What type of pass? The same factors are considered for every down and for every distance needed to make a first down.

In addition, the defensive coaches must consider how the weather conditions may alter the offensive planning and throughout the game must be constantly aware of the field position, the score, and the time remaining.

The actual defensive play to be used in any situation simplifies itself to a great degree since, for practical purposes, the offensive team has only a few options. They can run an inside play; they can run to their right side; they can run to their left side; they can throw a pass. The defensive coach decides what play he expects the offensive team to run and then calls the defense best able to stop that play.

For example, if the defensive coach expects the offense to run a play to the inside, he might call "pinch." With this call on a 3–2 set, the guards and tackles shoot their inside gap. The noseguard attacks the center. The inside linebackers "key" the block and movement of the offensive guards. On a 4–1 set, the guards and tackles shoot their inside gaps and the middle linebacker "keys" the

Basic defense to stop inside plays

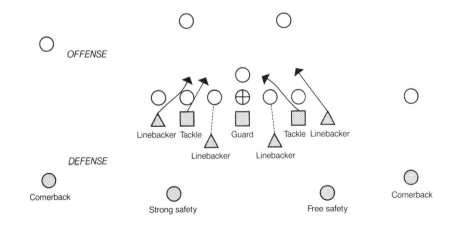

block of the offensive center. This defensive play should stop all inside plays either for no gain or a loss.

When the defensive coach expects a play to be run at the right side of his defense, he will signal "slant right." The tackles and the noseguard slant to the right. The outside linebacker on the right side crosses the line of scrimmage and places himself in position to turn the play to the inside. The inside linebackers "key" the movement and blocks of the offensive guards. That stunt should stop any play run to the defensive right side.

Basic defense to stop plays to the right side

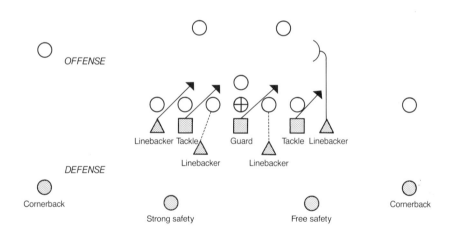

When the defensive coach expects the offense to run a play at the left side of his defense, he will signal "slant left." The down linemen and the linebackers would then perform the same stunt on the opposite side.

Basic defense to stop plays to the left side

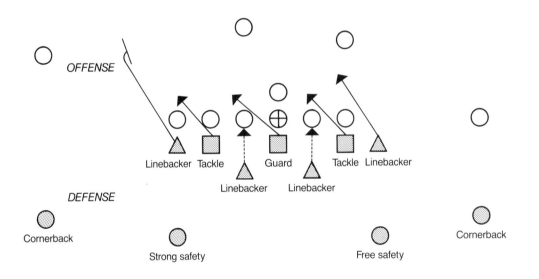

When the defensive coach expects a pass, he has two choices—either defend the pass by covering all receivers, or rush the passer in an attempt to get to him before the receivers have time to get open downfield.

When the defensive coach wants to cover the pass rather than put great pressure on the offensive quarterback with a rush, he will signal "cover." The tackles and noseguard rush the passer, but since only three men are rushing, usually the quarterback will have ample time to throw. But since the outside and inside linebackers, together with all the secondary men, are ready to drop back to cover every potential receiver, eight men are deployed to react to the ball when it is thrown.

When the defensive coach expects a pass and desires to put extreme pressure on the quarterback, he signals "blitz."

Pass defense to cover all receivers

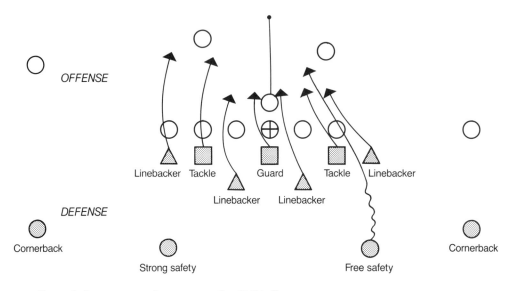

Pass defense to rush passer—the "blitz"

The objective of any blitz is to get a defensive man free to rush the passer before he can drop back and set up in position to throw the ball.

An effective blitz must be disguised so that the offensive team will not know that the linebackers and/or a safety may actually be rushing the passer. In an all-out blitz, there are no fewer than eight men rushing the passer.

The noseguard shoots the gap to the left side of the center. The left inside linebacker shoots the gap between the offensive guard and tackle to his side. The right inside linebacker shoots the gap between the center and the offensive guard to his side. The left defensive tackle shoots the gap to the outside of his offensive tackle. The right defensive tackle shoots the gap between the guard and tackle on his side. The left outside linebacker shoots outside of the offensive end. The right outside linebacker drives straight at the running back on his side.

The free safety, too, becomes a pass rusher. He takes his normal stance about seven yards behind the line of scrimmage. As the ball is snapped, he starts forward at full speed and goes through the gap between his tackle and linebacker.

The two cornerbacks and the strong safety play their normal three-deep zone pass defense—the cornerbacks each covering one-third of the field while the strong safety covers the middle third.

If the eight pass-rushers execute the charges as described, one of them— the most likely is the free safety—is almost certain to get to the quarterback before he can release the ball, or at least before he can pass it with any accuracy.

CHANGING THE ALIGNMENT

The defensive plays described above are simple and easy to execute. They put great pressure on the offensive team and might even result in fumbles or interceptions. A well-organized, poised offense will, however, be able to pick up defensive stunt plays. Therefore, to confuse the offensive blockers further, the defense can alter its alignment, requiring the offensive linemen to *readjust* their blocking assignments and increasing the possibility of their making a blocking mistake.

When the defensive coach decides to try to confuse the blockers, he will signal, "stack left." In the 3–2, the noseguard and the right interior lineman move a half step to their left, and line up in the gaps. The linebackers play directly behind them. From that alignment, down linemen can charge back to their original positions, shoot the gap in front of them, or charge to their right, while the linebackers step left and "key" the movement and blocks of the offensive guards.

How to confuse offensive blocking assignments by moving defensive linemen just before the ball is snapped—the "stack left"

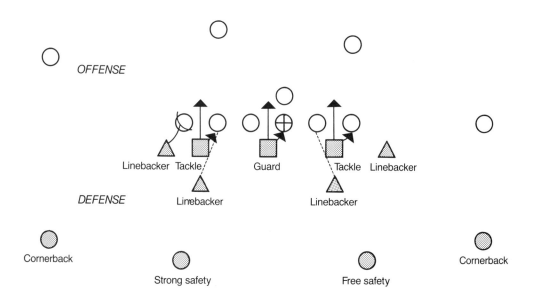

That adjustment—or its mirror image, "stack right"—does not require any time-consuming coaching or special preparation by the defensive team. Yet the "stack" alignments put great pressure on the offensive linemen since they are not sure which charge the defensive linemen will use.

Offensive teams always try to recognize the defensive alignment before they call the snap count. Offensive teams that take an inordinate amount of time to call the snap signal after setting up on the line of scrimmage usually are vulnerable to a quick change of alignment by the defense just before the snap signal is called. That is, after the offensive team has set in its formation, if the quarterback takes a long time to call a snap count, the defensive linebacker who calls the defensive plays to his teammates can call "left" or "right." When they hear that call, the linemen and inside linebackers move to the stack alignments described above. That change in alignment, after the offensive team has set and has recognized the initial defensive alignment, causes a readjustment of blocking assignments just before the ball is snapped. Almost always, this results in poor execution by the offensive team.

It should be noted that the same general defensive stunts can be used from the 4–1 alignment. On "pinch," the four down linemen shoot the gaps to their inside. On "left," the four down linemen slant to the left. On "right," the four down linemen slant to their right. On "cover," the four down linemen rush the passer while the remaining seven men cover their defensive pass coverage zones. On "blitz," the four down linemen, linebackers, and the strong safety rush while the cornerbacks and the free safety play man-for-man pass defense.

ADJUSTING THE DEFENSE AGAINST MEN IN MOTION AND FORMATION CHANGES

After setting up at the line of scrimmage, the offense can easily change its formation by using a man in motion. The man in motion is usually a wide receiver who, after the offensive team is ready to put the ball in play, moves across the field to the opposite side. The cornerback assigned to him must move across the field with him to be in position to play either a zone or man-for-man should a pass play be used. If the play is a run, the defensive man immediately reacts to the play and supports against the ballcarrier.

Since the cornerback is moving laterally, and since the two safeties are likely to think "pass defense" rather than "run defense," the movement of the wide receiver in motion weakens the ability of the secondary men to support as effectively against a running play as they can if there is no man in motion to distract them.

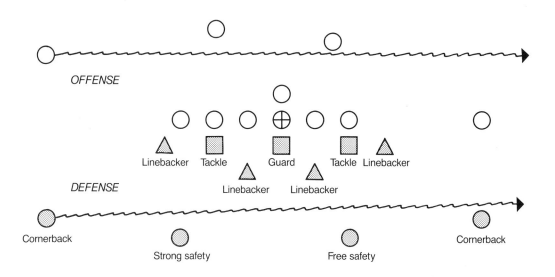

OFFENSE

Linebacker Tackle Guard Tackle Linebacker

DEFENSE

Linebacker Linebacker

Cornerback

Strong safety Free safety

Cornerback

Adjusting the defense when a man on offense goes in motion before the ball is snapped
Here the left defensive cornerback covers the man in motion.

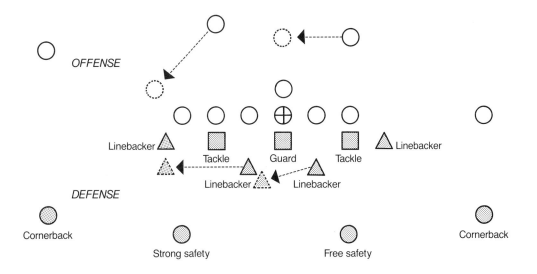

OFFENSE

Linebacker Tackle Guard Tackle Linebacker

Linebacker Linebacker

DEFENSE

Cornerback

Strong safety Free safety

Cornerback

Adjusting the defense when the offensive backs change their positions before the ball is snapped

An additional problem for the defense is a change of position by the offensive backs after they have taken their original set. The new formation will have a different basic strength. The defensive team must adjust to it.

Since those changes usually require the movement of only the two running backs, the linebackers automatically adjust to the new position of the backs. The linebackers have been told in practice exactly where to line up against each formation of the running backs. Thus, the linebackers, having taken their positions against the original formation, must be poised to move with the running backs to be in the best alignment against the new formation created by a fast shift.

Of course, it is possible to have the signal-calling linebacker call one of the defenses discussed above. But since the ball is usually snapped within two seconds after the backs have shifted, there is usually not enough time to have the entire defensive team hear a new call and react. Also, there is no guarantee that on any down the backs will not shift two or three times to different formations before the ball is actually snapped. If the linebackers are trying to call an entirely new defense for each shift, it would become totally confusing to the defensive team.

To compound the defense's difficulties, it is also possible for the offense to put one of the running backs in motion prior to the snap of the ball. If that occurs, the defense must adjust. How? Since the linebackers usually have the coverage responsibility against the running backs, the linebacker to the side where the motion occurs moves with the in-motion running back to be in position to cover him if the play is a pass, or to support quickly if a running play is used.

SUMMARY

As noted at the outset of the book, it is much more difficult to play defense than offense. Before the ball is snapped, the offensive players know if a man will go in motion, if the backs will change formation, what the final formation will be. Also, they know whom they are supposed to block in every possible defensive set.

The defense knows none of that. When the offensive team breaks the huddle and moves to the line of scrimmage, defensive men take their positions for the defense called. Then they must adjust to any changes in formation or to men in motion and they must defeat the opponent attempting to block them even though the offensive team, knowing the count, will have a slight jump. The defense must also ignore all fakes and move to the ball and stop the play. All of that requires quick decision-making ability and fast reactions to each situation.

Anyone with physical skills can be taught to play effectively on offense. It takes a fine athlete with the reactions of a master detective to play effectively on defense.

Preparing the Game Plan

Any offensive play, whether a pass or a run, always looks successful in the diagram. Fortunately for the defense, there is a marked difference between a play as it is diagrammed and as it is executed by an offensive team.

Moreover, in preparing their offense, teams usually seek perfect balance between their running and passing attacks. In reality, though, such perfection is rarely the case. Indeed, the offensive team, when carefully analyzed, will always have definite strengths and weaknesses, which are determined by the skills of their personnel.

In preparing their game plan, the defensive team should make it their major objective to *stop what their opponents do best.* It is a truism that "the defense should force the offense to try to successfully run plays they have never used effectively in previous games."

ANALYZING THE OPPONENT'S RUNNING GAME

The opponent's offensive team will usually use two or more formations. They may also use men in

The best defensive teams are always prepared to stop what their opponents do best.

By analyzing scouting reports and game films, defensive coaches discover tender-
cies and weaknesses in their opponents' offensive game.

motion or make formation adjustments after taking their original position
Using films and scouting reports, defensive coaches should analyze their oppo
nent's point of attack on all running plays from each formation they have use
Let's say, for example, that the scouting report indicates that the opponent
offensive team has never run a play to the outside of the split end. Obviousl
the defensive plan should be designed to stop all plays from the offensive cent
to outside of the tight end.

Granted, that is a pretty clear-cut example, but scouting reports and cha
analysis can reveal even the subtle tendencies of an opponent's offense, and tl
defense can then be set up to stop those plays that have been successful for tl
opponent from their favorite formations.

The same kind of defensive planning is used in stopping the individual opponent's passing game. Once again, an opponent's formations are charted from films and scouting reports, and now it will be clear where the ball has been thrown from each formation. Below are a pair of charts showing the passes that have been thrown from two offensive formations. In Chart A, it is immediately apparent that the short outside patterns must be defended at all times. In Chart B, it is apparent that the defense must be designed to stop deep passes directed at the right side of the defense.

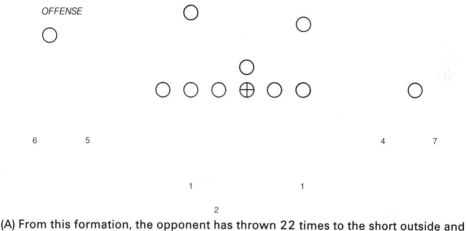

(A) From this formation, the opponent has thrown 22 times to the short outside and only twice downfield deep.

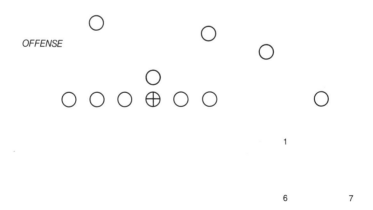

(B) From this formation, the opponent has thrown 13 times to the deep right side of the defense and only once to the short right side.

The defensive plan should also take into consideration the timing of the passes used by the offensive team. If the offense throws mostly from the three-step quarterback drop, linebackers should play deeper and the secondary closer, since most of the time the ball will be delivered quickly. If the offensive team normally throws from a five-step or a seven-step drop by the quarterback, the linebackers and secondary can play their normal distance from the line of scrimmage and react and read their keys as they normally do, because they will have time, before the ball is thrown, to move to their designated areas of coverage.

ADJUSTING THE DEFENSE AFTER THE START OF THE GAME

As a rule, the defensive alignment at the start of the game should be one that has not been used or shown in previous games. That can bewilder the offensive team. After all, during its practices in the week before the game, the offense has worked against the defensive alignments previously used. When on the first play of the game, the offensive team breaks the huddle, gets to the line of scrimmage, tries to recognize the defense, and sees an alignment that it has *not* practiced against, confusion arises and confidence is sapped. The individual offensive player thinks: "Our coaching staff has been outsmarted. We haven't practiced against this defense!" Meanwhile, the opposing coaches, both in the press box and in the sideline, are surprised by the new alignment. They immediately must divert their attention from the flow of the game while they decide what plays they think can be run effectively against the new defensive set.

The defensive team should stay in the new alignment as long as it is successful. When the offensive team adjusts to it and begins to move the ball, the defensive team should return to its normal defensive plays and formations.

By using the new alignment, the defensive team has accomplished two things: It has shaken the offensive team's confidence in its coaches and its own ability to score against the new defensive alignment, and it has forced the offensive coaches to spend their time and attention on adjusting to the new defense. And while that damage is being inflicted, the defensive team can sow further confusion by returning to their standard alignments and stunts!

When a defensive team does return to its normal defenses, its coaches should carefully analyze what plays are being run successfully on particular down and yardage situations, and then use the defensive stunts that will stop these plays.

Offensive teams almost always repeat plays that have been successful in particular down and yardage situations. For example, if the team has successfully run inside plays on short yardage situations, the next time that down and yardage situation occurs, the defense should call the "pinch" stunt. If on previous third-and-long yardage situations the offensive team has been consistently successful in throwing long passes, the defensive coach should call "blitz." That defensive play will place great pressure on the passer and make it virtually impossible for him to complete a long throw downfield.

To make those kinds of situational adjustments, defensive coaches must keep meticulous records of the plays an opponent is running successfully in certain down and yardage situations.

BUILDING MORALE

Usually there is a key back or pass receiver on the opposition who must be stopped if the defense is to be successful.

In practice, the "scout team"—the team that in practice is running the formations and plays of the opponent—should have the players wear the same numbers as the key opposing players to be faced. That will familiarize the defensive team with their particular opponents, give the defense specific men on whom to focus their attention, and help motivate them.

Practice should be organized so that the defensive coaches know what play will be run each time against the defense. That enables them to call the defensive play, or stunt, that will be most effective against the play being run. Repetition of the appropriate stunt for each play builds the defensive team's confidence that it *can* and *will* be able to stop the opponent.

The coaching staff should always be honest with their team regarding the offensive strength of the opponent. When the opponent possesses a truly great offense (they are, say, the statistical leaders of the conference in all offensive categories) the coaching staff must condition the players mentally not to be overly concerned if the offensive team makes a series of first downs. They simply explain to the defense that in all probability the opponent's offense will move the ball.

The team is taught to adopt the "bend-but-not-break" defensive philosophy, which means that the players remain confident that the defensive unit will not allow a breakaway touchdown play by either a pass or a run and that they will never allow a single play to gain over 15 yards. Those objectives are attainable.

A goal-line stand puts the "bend-but-not-break" philosophy to its sternest test.

The most consistent statistic in football at any level is that the offensive team will get the ball on an exchange of possession 14 times during any game. The defensive team knows that the opponent's offense may be penalized, fumble the ball, or miss offensive assignments. Whenever any of those things occur, the offense will be unable to make a first down. They will have to give up the ball.

By properly understanding the "bend-but-not-break" philosophy, the defensive team gains confidence that it will be able to limit the opponent's scoring. The defensive team should keep track of the number of times it has stopped the opponents and forced them to give up the ball. After the first possession, the defensive players know that they need only stop them 13 more times, then 12, 11, and so on. If the opponent occasionally puts points on the board, the defensive team can gain heart by recognizing the number of times they now need to stop the opponent before the game ends. Meanwhile, they must be taught to believe that their offensive team has the ability to put more points on the board than they have given up to their opponent's offense.

Practice Schedules

A recurring myth in football is that there is a "game player." The myth would have us believe that on game day, a player, because of the enthusiasms of the moment, rises above himself and performs better than he ever has in practice. In my long experience in football, I have never seen a "game player."

Repetitive practice is the only way a player can learn to perform effectively. When the ball is snapped, defensive players do not have time to think. Instead, they must instinctively react to the play being run.

To teach each player to react accurately, the coaching staff, during practice, must *create every situation* the defensive player will face in a game. The player then repeats his reaction to each situation until he can respond perfectly.

To create every situation the players will face requires meticulous planning by the coaching staff. If an opposing offense uses any maneuver that the defensive players have not practiced against, it will probably be successful. The fault lies with the defensive coaching staff, not with the players. They have not been properly prepared.

It is a long, tedious, difficult assignment for each player to be totally prepared to meet every

155

The best practice sessions duplicate game situations.

possible situation. However, it is the only way players can truly be considered ready to play. There are no "game players." There are only men who, through diligent practice, are at their peak.

The practice time allowed for high school and college teams is governed by conference and national rules. Obviously, professional teams have unlimited practice time.

Colleges and high schools usually have three separate times of practice—spring, early fall, and in-season practice every week to prepare for the next opponent.

From a coaching standpoint, spring practice has two objectives. Players must be taught to execute effectively the fundamentals of their particular position, and the skills of each player must be analyzed and evaluated so that each man is assigned to play the position in which he can best use his talents. All men work on agility drills, block protection, and tackling techniques. In addition, linebackers and secondary men work on man-for-man and zone pass defense, while the down linemen work on their pass-rush skills.

In early fall practice, the players sharpen their execution of the fundamentals of their position and the coaching staff reevaluates the positions assigned to each man on the defensive team. Any player who is "out of position" and has the skills to play better elsewhere should be moved to the new position. For example, if a cornerback lacks the speed to cover a swift wide receiver, he should be moved to one of the safety positions. Likewise, an outside linebacker who lacks the quickness to be an effective pass defender should be moved to inside linebacker, where his pass coverage skill is not as important as his ability to stop running plays.

During in-season practice, sessions should be designed so that the players can familiarize themselves with the expected offensive plays of the upcoming opponent.

In all three periods of practice, meticulously timed planning is a must. Amateur players, in addition to learning to play football, must keep up with their school work and family and social responsibilities. On the average, each player can daily devote no more than three hours—including time necessary to be taped and dressed—to football practice. Demands on athletes' time are even more severe at the military service academies. Because of the rigorous daily schedules of those schools, football players can only devote 1 hour and 45 minutes a day, including dressing time, to football practice.

To best utilize the limited time available for practice, the coaching staff should conduct position and group meetings with the team before anyone goes to the practice field. At these meetings, the players are told exactly *what* they will do in each drill and *how* they will execute each drill. By knowing what is expected of them, players become ready to execute their various drills as soon as they reach the field, and the coaches can devote themselves to correcting any errors that occur.

It is a serious mistake for coaches *not* to explain in meetings what will occur at practice before the team goes out on the field. Teaching the players what to do and how to react can be done better in a classroom situation. When on the practice field, players often have difficulty hearing, since they are wearing helmets and the wind may be blowing. And they may be out of breath and unable to concentrate on coaches' instructions because of the physical effort they have made in the previous drill.

The attitude of the players toward practice is obviously a key factor in the improvement of the team. The coaching staff must teach each player that the only purpose of practice is to improve the ability of the individual players on the team. Players must be taught to make an all-out effort in every drill during practice. That results in a habit of total effort, which transforms itself into total effort on every play in a game.

Fans and coaches often talk about the importance of the "will to win." Of course, that is important on game day. But unless the team has had the much more important "will to prepare," their desire to win will be unimportant.

It is easy for each man to be emotionally high on game day. The stands are full, the bands are playing, parents and friends are watching.

The tough testing time of a team's "will to prepare" is the morning practice on the fifth day of the two-a-day practice sessions in early fall. The players are tired and bruised. They would prefer not to practice. But if they simply live through the session with the thought of getting it over as soon as possible, they will not improve. If they have the true "will to prepare," they will execute each drill with an all-out effort. Through that personal discipline—a total best effort in each drill—players develop the habit of always doing their best.

In general, coaches should talk to players at the start of practice and then devote the rest of the practice schedule to improving the players' skills and techniques. After all, practice is for practicing, not for listening to lectures.

Besides learning the needed skills and techniques, players should be taught the basic defenses the team will use throughout the season. Then the defensive stunts should be learned, followed by the goal-line defense, the prevent defense, and the defensive kicking plays. Through the teaching progression, all elements of the team's defensive play are assimilated.

A week before the first game, practice should be planned to prepare the team for the opponent to be played. The usual drills remain a part of practice, but greater emphasis should now be placed on preparing for an opponent's probable offensive plan.

Players will practice diligently until they feel comfortably confident of their assignments against an upcoming opponent and are confident they can execute the assignments with ease. When a player reaches that point mentally, further practice is unnecessary. Indeed, he may lose valuable incentive and purpose if drilled further. Thus, coaches should plan practice schedules carefully so that for a game being played on Saturday, no player is totally comfortable about his preparation until the end of practice on Thursday.

Coaches should also realize that as the season progresses, less time need be spent on fundamentals. When a player has been through spring and early fall practice and played half of the regular season, he will be about as capable a fundamental player as he can possibly be during the season in progress. At that point, grueling practice sessions are foolish. Instead, practice should be shortened and generally designed to maintain fundamental skills while simultaneously preparing the team for its next opponent.

WEEKLY PRACTICE SCHEDULES

The following practice schedules assume that the team played a game the previous Saturday and that the players are available for practice at 3:15 in the afternoon. The period between 3:15 and 3:30, when normal practice begins, will be used to "loosen up" and give the specialty men—kickers, holders, punters—an opportunity to work on their skills.

Monday

3:30   Stretching and warm-up exercises.

3:40   Players who participated in the game on Saturday will be in sweatsuits. They will come together as a team to practice the new defensive plays and stunts that will be used in the coming game. A comfortable amount of time to allow for that is about 20 minutes. When the period is over, those players should run two or three laps around the field and return to the dressing room to shower and change. Players who did not play in the game on Saturday should scrimmage against an offensive team for about 30 minutes. That will maintain their "real-game" skills and keep them in a "hitting mood."

3:30   Stretching and warm-up exercises.

3:40   Isolated group work. The defensive linemen, linebackers, and secondary men each work in a separate group to practice their skills and techniques.

4:00   The linebackers and secondary men join to practice pass defense. The defensive linemen continue their group work.

4:25   The defensive team joins together and practices the defenses to be used against the coming opponent.

5:00   Practice punt defenses and returns.

5:10   Practice field goal defense.

5:20   Practice kickoff coverage and onside kicks.

5:30   End of practice.

Wednesday

3:30   Stretching and warm-up exercises.

3:40   Isolated group work.

3:55   The linebackers and secondary men join to practice pass defense. The defensive linemen continue their group work.

4:20   The defensive team joins together and practices the defenses to be used against the coming opponent.

4:50   Practice punt defenses and returns.

5:00   Practice field goal defense.

5:10   Practice kickoff coverage and onside kicks.

5:20   End of practice.

Thursday

3:30   Stretching and warm-up exercises.

3:35   Isolated group work.

3:45   The linebackers and secondary men join to practice pass defense. The defensive linemen continue their isolated group work.

4:05   The defensive team joins together and practices the defenses to be used against the coming opponent.

4:35   Practice punt defenses and returns.

4:45   Practice field goal defense.

4:55   Practice kickoff coverage and onside kicks.

5:05   End of practice.

3:30   Stretching and warm-up exercises.

3:35   Defensive teamwork emphasizing short yardage and goal-line defenses.

3:55   Review punt defenses and punt returns.

4:05   Review kickoff coverage and onside kicks.

4:15   Review field-goal-block-kick plays and defense.

4:25   End of practice.

PHYSICAL CONDITIONING

Through learning and executing the "will to prepare," players will achieve the physical conditioning needed to perform well. In addition to the physical and mental work during practice, players must understand the vital importance of eating a well-balanced diet and getting enough sleep and rest to achieve and maintain prime physical condition.

At the college and professional levels, players eat at a training table. Their diet is designed to provide the needed calories and proper balance of dairy products, meats, fish, fowl, vegetables, and salads.

Players at the high school level and below do not have training tables and must eat the food provided by their families. At the beginning of spring practice and again in the fall, high school coaches should arrange a meeting with the parents of all men on the team. At this meeting, parents are told, in depth, how the football program will be operated, how their sons will be coached, what their diet should be, and how much rest they will need. The parents should be asked to cooperate in assisting their sons to develop the proper mental attitude and achieve their top potential as players.

Different families have varying economic resources. While a well-balanced diet is desirable for every player, some families do not have the needed income to provide, on a continuing basis, well-planned "training table" meals. At the parents' meeting, coaches should show the parents ways to provide an adequately balanced diet for their sons even though they may not have large financial resources. Cereals, for example, are inexpensive and contain most of the vitamins and fiber needed in a balanced diet. Many vegetables are inexpensive and, when properly prepared, quite nutritious. Eggs are a relatively cheap form of protein, and fresh fruits in season are inexpensive and complete the needed food requirements for a football player's diet.

Parents should also be instructed about a desired lights-out schedule for

their sons. Under normal circumstances, parents should be asked to see that
their sons are in bed by 10:30 each night. The boys will be tired from practice.
By retiring at this hour, they will have sufficient time to get their needed amount
of rest.

GAME-DAY PREPARATION

Teams usually play their games in the afternoon or at night. In either case, the
same general schedule should be followed:

Players should eat a pre-game meal 3½ hours before the game will begin.
That will ensure that the meal is digested properly and that players will not
become hungry before the game has ended.

The team should have a final meeting two hours before the game. At the
session, coaches should re-emphasize all phases of the defensive game plan and
remind each man, one last time, what he must do in each situation to play
effectively.

After the meeting, players report to the locker room to be properly taped
for the contest.

The team should go on the field for warm-up drills about 40 minutes before
the kickoff. That will give them ample time to prepare themselves physically
and leave enough time for a short pre-game pep talk by the coaches before
returning to the field for the kickoff.

SUMMARY

Another recurring myth about football is that coaches can deliver a rousing pep
talk to the team before the game—or at halftime—which somehow remarkably
makes the team more effective than they have ever been.

In practical terms, unless the team has had the "will to prepare," no
last-minute exhortations on the part of the coach can dramatically affect the
team's performance.

Players must learn during spring practice and early fall practice how to
play the game and they must develop the habit of making their best effort at
all times. If those objectives have not been achieved, the team will never be able
to perform to its potential. If the twin objectives have been achieved, the team
can always play to its fullest capability.

An intricate part of each player's self-understanding should be that, for

The great player is the one who plays to his fullest potential.

practical purposes, *he is playing against himself*—not against an opponent.

In some games, a player may face an opponent of superior physical skills. The important factor is not how often the player handles his opponent effectively. Instead, the only thing that matters is that the player makes his best effort on every play.

In other games the player will face a physically inferior opponent. Again, the player must gauge his performance not on how many times he easily handled his opponent. Instead, the constant remains: Did he perform on each play to the full extent of his ability?

When the entire team has every man making his best effort on every play, regardless of the ability of the opponent faced, the team will have achieved the objective of playing to its full potential.

How to Watch Defensive Football

Fans attend football games to enjoy the colorful crowd, pageantry, and bands as well as the game itself. The enjoyment of simply being there often is more important to the spectator than the game itself.

For many fans, sophisticated modern football appears to be too confusing to understand in any technical, strategic sense. The players are obviously excellent athletes. One team has the ball and the other team doesn't. Both teams are using well-practiced plays, but why they do precisely what they do is not understood by the average spectator.

Everyone who attends a football game would enjoy the spectacle more, I think, with a basic knowledge of how the game is played. As in any learning process, that requires a small amount of study and understanding.

Since the movement of the ball is always easy to see, and since it is the object of the game to get the ball across the goal line for a touchdown or to kick a field goal when the kicker is in range, most spectators are content simply to follow the ball instead of expanding their knowledge to comprehend why the offensive team uses the formations and plays that it does and why the defensive team

When watching a football game, try not to watch the ball.

deploys as it does to counter the play of the offensive team.

In previous chapters, we have described the basic offensive formations used in modern football: the "T" formation; the Pro set; the "I" formation; three wide receivers; and four wide receivers. We have also carefully examined how and why the defense adjusts to the offensive formations.

Knowledge of offensive formations is vital to a sound understanding of the game. When the offensive team breaks the huddle, what is its offensive set? How many wide receivers are being used? How many running backs are in position to carry the ball? It is also helpful to understand the defenses used in modern football, which are described in this book.

It requires discipline and practice on the part of the spectator to watch a football game intelligently. The basic fundamental the fan must learn is *not to watch the ball.* Instead, he should, in order:

1. Recognize the offensive formation being used
2. Note the number of defensive down linemen
3. Note the number of defensive linebackers
4. Recognize the pattern of the defensive secondary

The Five Basic Offensive Formations in Modern Football

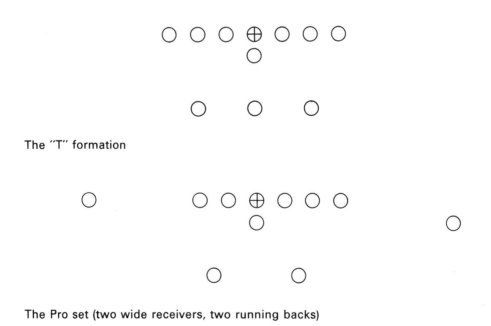

The "T" formation

The Pro set (two wide receivers, two running backs)

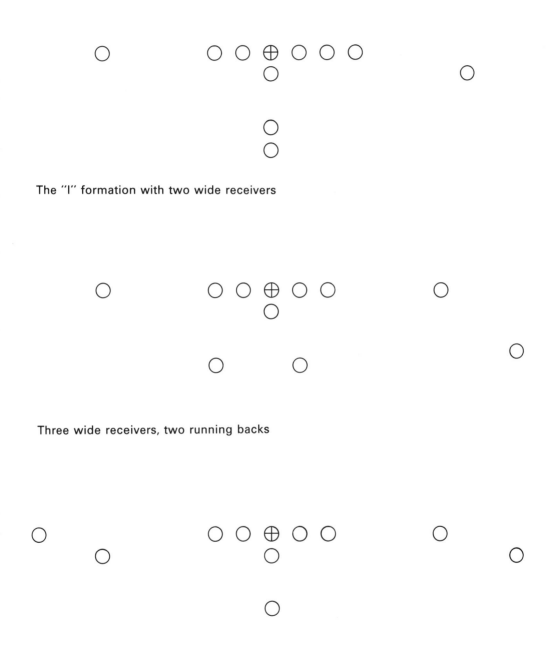

The "I" formation with two wide receivers

Three wide receivers, two running backs

Four wide receivers, one running back

After recognizing the offensive formation, the spectator should count the number of down linemen and the number of linebackers and should note the pattern of the defensive secondary.

The spectator who mentally notes those four points in the order listed will know *before the ball is snapped* both the offensive formation being used *and* the defensive alignment against it. Is the interior defensive alignment the 4–1 or the 3–2? Is the secondary the regular two cornerbacks and two safeties or is it a "monster" alignment? Is the defense playing a "prevent" defense or a goal-line defense?

When the ball is snapped, what would have seemed to be a confusing melee of players now takes on a certain shape and order as the spectator begins to understand what the defense is trying to accomplish on the play being run.

As the play develops, the defensive spectator should train himself to make the following observations: How did the defensive linemen charge? Did they slant to one side or the other? Did they shoot the inside gaps?

Did the linebackers read their keys and simply react to the play being run or did they penetrate across the line of scrimmage or start immediately to drop back to be in position to cover a pass?

How did the secondary play? On a running play, did they quickly support at the point of attack? If the offensive team is showing pass, are the secondary men playing a zone or a man-for-man defense? Did either safety or a cornerback immediately leave his position on a blitz?

As you read this, it still may seem complex and confusing. With just a little discipline and practice, however, you can learn to see the play develop as described.

Again, the cardinal rule is *not to watch the ball.* By watching the defensive team's alignments, you can learn to recognize their patterns of play and, gradually, as you watch the defense react to the play being run, the ball will become the focal point of your attention.

WATCHING DEFENSIVE FOOTBALL ON TELEVISION

For most of the past 20 years I have worked as a "color commentator" for televised football games. The play-by-play announcer is responsible for describing the play and reporting who carries, throws, or catches the ball and who makes the tackle or breaks up the pass play. As the color announcer, I am responsible after the play-by-play announcer has described the play to explain *why the offensive play was successful or why it failed.* Time permitting—and that is always a problem—I try to explain why the offensive team is using its tactics and strategy and how the defense is attempting to adjust to the offensive plays.

The major problem every color announcer faces is the difference between what he can see by watching the entire field of play and what the home viewer can see on his own screen.

Television cameras rarely show much of the defensive team. Usually the viewer can see the defensive linemen and occasionally the inside linebackers. Rarely does he see any of the defensive secondary men until well after the play begins.

In the announcer's booth, we have a TV monitor that shows us the picture you see at home. I have taught myself, before the ball is snapped, to watch the entire field. At the moment the ball is snapped, I look at our booth TV so that I will be able to comment on what the viewer has seen and avoid mentioning anything he has not seen.

Before the ball is snapped, the viewer should first identify the offensive formation being used. The camera always shows the offensive linemen and the position of the running backs. Usually it does not show wide receivers. The viewer can make an easy mathematical calculation, though: If a tight end and

When watching football on television, fans should first identify the offensive formation being used, then the positions of the defensive linemen and visible linebackers.

two running backs are in the game, there will be two wide receivers; if a tight end and one running back are in the game, there will be three wide receivers; if no tight end and two running backs are in the game, there will be three wide receivers; and if no tight end and only one running back is in the game, there will be four wide receivers.

Before the ball is snapped and after the viewer has identified the offensive formation being used, he should focus his attention on the down linemen and their precise position. Are there three or four down linemen? Are they playing head-up with their opponents or in the gaps? If the viewer can see the interior linebackers, is there only one or are there two? That will enable the viewer to know whether the interior set is a 4–1 or a 3–2. How deep are the linebackers playing? That will give the viewer a hint as to whether the linebackers will read their keys normally or be involved in a forcing stunt.

As the ball is snapped, the viewer should try to watch the charges of the defensive down linemen and the linebackers. As the play progresses, the viewer notes which defensive men first appear on the screen as they react to the play. That will enable the viewer to understand quickly the defensive pattern being used, even though the cameras do not show the entire defensive team as the play begins.

To watch as described requires a little study of offensive formations and defensive patterns. Thereupon, the viewer must discipline himself to watch the play in the progression described. If he can do so, the result is a far greater enjoyment of the game—the viewer can see, recognize, and understand why and how the game is being played.

Last Words

In the past few years defensive football has changed a great deal. More changes can be expected because the defense must always adjust to the formations and plays used by the offensive team, and football offenses are constantly being revised.

When football was a one-platoon game, offensive teams did not have great versatility. Rarely did they possess a fine passing attack. Mainly, they relied on their ability to run the football.

Two-platoon football radically changed offensive thinking. Players with the skill to throw and catch the ball became increasingly proficient and passing attacks increasingly complex.

In today's game, the defense realizes it must play effectively against the running attack and at all times be ready to defend well against a versatile, well-designed passing attack.

A further refinement by today's defensive teams is the expanded use of the free substitution rule, so that the proper players are always in the game to defend against the play most likely to be run by the offensive team, no matter what the down and yardage situation. In fact, nowadays, the only time the defensive team plays its starting

Expanded use of the free substitution rule has greatly refined defensive play.

No matter how sophisticated the level of play may become, good defense will always be a team effort.

personnel is on first and ten, second down and five or six, or third down and three or four.

The rest of the time, defensive coaches will substitute. On short-yardage situations they put additional linemen in the game. On long-yardage situations, one or two pass defenders will enter the game to strengthen the pass defense.

I cannot emphasize enough that excellent defense is the key to victory. A team must stop the opponent and gain possession of the ball before it can use its own offense. The only other way the team can get possession is by allowing the offense to score and then receive a kickoff. Teams rarely win by getting the ball that way.

The offense possesses the initiative. Its men know what formation will be used, what play will be run, and the moment the ball will be snapped. Thus, the defensive team is at a disadvantage when each play begins. It requires great athletic skill and preparation on the part of all members of the defense to overcome those disadvantages and still stop the play.

Most of the publicity and glamour surrounding a football team is focused on offensive players—particularly the quarterback, running backs, and the pass receivers. The coaching staff must understand and accept the challenge that presents regarding the placement of personnel on the offensive and defensive teams. If great defensive play is the key to victory, obviously the best athletes on the team should be assigned to the defensive squad.

The coaching staff must explain and the squad must understand that truth. Perhaps the best way of putting it is that the offensive players are *not in the game* until the team gets possession of the ball. When the best athletes are assigned to offense, while the opponent has the ball they are sitting on the bench. When they are not participating in the game, they cannot make any contribution to help their team win.

Players know and recognize that the most publicized players will be the men on the offensive team—particularly those who are involved in throwing, running, and catching the ball. Players relish the personal recognition they receive, and it is normal for them to want to play offense. Each player must be taught, however, to subordinate his own selfish interests and play the position where he can make his greatest contribution to the success of the team.

That is one reason football is such a fascinating game. The men who are the most responsible for winning or losing—the linemen—rarely get much attention or notice. The headlines and glory go to the publicized offensive stars. Yet to win, the unnoticed, unpublicized men must perform with maximum effectiveness.

Fans are beginning to better understand the importance and value of defense. I suspect that this understanding and appreciation will grow in the years ahead and perhaps one day, defensive players will finally receive the accolades they deserve.

Until then, all defensive teams should realize that when they have held an opponent scoreless or limited them to only 7 or 10 points, they have much to be proud of! They can say—and their offensive teammates should know—that their performance on defense was the most important ingredient in achieving the victory.